CICS

A Practical Guide to
System Fine Tuning

CICS

A Practical Guide to System Fine Tuning

Stephen Piggott

Intertext Publications
McGraw-Hill Book Company
New York   St. Louis   San Francisco   Aukland   Bogota
Hamburg   London   Madrid   Mexico City   Milan   Montreal
New Delhi   Panama City   Paris   Sao Paulo
Singapore   Sydney   Tokyo   Toronto

To the memory of my late father, Thomas,
to my mother, Olive, and to my wife, June.

Library of Congress Catalog Card Number 88-83061

10 9 8 7 6 5 4 3 2 1

ISBN 0-07-050054-1

Intertext Publications/Multiscience Press, Inc.
One Lincoln Plaza
New York, NY 10023

McGraw-Hill Book Company
1221 Avenue of the Americas
New York, NY 10020

Composed in Ventura Publisher by Context, Inc.

Contents

Acknowledgments

The source for the ideas presented in this book, other than my own, are acknowledged in the Bibliography section at the end. I should like to add my own personal appreciation to these authors and all others who take the time and trouble to share their professional experiences with their fellows and who ultimately enhance the understanding of us all. Their often selfless actions are responsible for much of the progress achieved in the world of Data Processing today.

I would like to gratefully acknowledge the part that Jay Ranade, my Editor-in-Chief, has played in the production of this book. Not only has he patiently and carefully guided me through the various stages of its production, but he has also made a significant number of suggestions for its improvement.

My thanks are also extended to the management and staff of my employers, Xephon Technology Transfer Ltd, particularly the Managing Director, Chris Bunyan, for both their practical assistance and constant encouragement.

On a more personal note, I would like to express my gratitude to my Friday night drinking companions, Pat Kersey and Mike Rawlings, for uncannily knowing when I needed to be left alone and when I should be dragged from my word processor.

Thanks are also due to my three children, Laura, Melanie, and Nicholas, for, mostly anyway, leaving me to work at home undisturbed and for showing a maturity beyond their years in understanding why Daddy couldn't play with them.

I should like to thank all my friends and relations for their continuous encouragement and support throughout the time I was working on this book. Outstanding in this respect was my late father-in-law, Fred Goodright, who sadly will not see my ideas become a reality.

Finally, a word of thanks to my wife, June, who has not only given me her tremendous support throughout but who was always on hand to provide me with refreshment and nourishment. If behind every great man there is a great woman, my future success looks assured.

Preface

It was during my years as a CICS systems programmer, at the sharp end of IBM software so to speak, that I first became acquainted with a dilemma that thousands of others in similar positions must have faced. It was how to maintain the performance of existing systems in the face of continuing change and increased workloads. What was particularly irritating was the lack of good concise reading material to help me find an ounce or so of extra processing capacity from aging software and hardware.

Like many others, I had many niggling doubts in my mind that perhaps I had not always selected the values best suited to my installation's needs when I had gone about the job of choosing CICS table parameter settings. But which of the many would benefit most from being changed? Which ones were ideally defined, albeit more by luck than judgment? Was it a good use of my time to research all the values anyway? Where could my time best be used to give the maximum return from the minimum outlay? If I had known then that I was not alone in looking for the answers to these questions, this book would have been written a good deal earlier.

Instead, I persevered and little by little the muddy waters cleared until a brighter picture emerged and some sort of a basis from which I could start tuning was born. My early efforts had mixed results. I don't think that I ever worsened performance, but there were certainly times when a lot of frantic effort was rewarded by a lack of any measurable improvement.

My later experiences in consultancy and as the editor of a CICS technical journal have given me a whole new perspective on what I was doing wrong in those far-off days and I have drawn heavily on those experiences in compiling this book. If it's true that one learns from one's mistakes, then I could be overqualified to be the author of this book.

Foreword

IBM's ubiquitous Customer Information Control System (CICS) has been one of its major software triumphs and, with the announcement of its participation in IBM's Systems Application Architecture strategy, its role in the world of information technology looks more significant than ever. But along with an increased dependence on CICS systems comes a reduced tolerance to their failure to provide timely response. And so it becomes more and more important for management and technicians alike to appreciate the key factors that affect CICS performance and understand the fine balance that has to be struck in improving one part of the system without unduly worsening another. CICS Performance is based, not only on the author Steve Piggott's own personal experiences as a systems programmer with a large multi-national company, but on the contacts he has made with hundreds of technical personnel all over the world in his position as editor of CICS Update, a monthly journal for CICS users. Pooling knowledge from so many varied sources CICS Performance is able:

- to assess the implications of the full range of options available when selecting parameters for CICS tables.
- to explain the full performance implications of various aspects of application design.
- to descibe how to reduce response times through a better understanding of CICS and VSAM file handling methods.
- to examine ways of optimizing the workload on the terminal network.
- to offer the basis of a methodology for improving and controlling the performance of a CICS system. CICS Performance is an ex-

perience-based volume that will prove invaluable to the newcomer and veteran alike. It is written in a "no nonsense" manner with few frills, attacking the subjects crucial to improving CICS performance head on. This is certainly a book that nobody with any interest at all in CICS performance should be without.

1

Introduction

This chapter takes a look at CICS today and looks back at how it has evolved over the years to reach the position of dominance that it enjoys today. The author reveals how the role of the systems programmer has had to develop to keep up with this rapid evolution. This chapter also advises the reader on how to concentrate any tuning effort on those areas where it will achieve the best possible effects.

CICS Evolution

It is doubtful whether even IBM could have predicted the impact that CICS would have when it was revealed to an unsuspecting audience in 1968. Software marketing has never been the company's strong suit, and with a great deal of uncertainty it opted for a "blanket" approach and offered a product that was "all things to all men."

1968	CICS Type II
1969	CICS/OS Version 1
1970	CICS/DOS Version 1
1971	CICS/OS Version 2
1973	CICS/OS/VS 1.0.0 CICS/DOS/VS 1.0.0
1974	CICS/OS/VS 1.1.0 CICS/DOS/VS 1.1.0
1975	CICS/OS/VS 1.1.1 CICS/DOS/VS 1.1.1
1976	CICS/OS/VS 1.2.0 CICS/DOS/VS 1.2.0
1977	CICS/OS/VS 1.3.0 CICS/DOS/VS 1.3.0
1978	CICS/OS/VS 1.4.0 CICS/DOS/VS 1.4.0 CICS/OS/VS 1.4.1 CICS/DOS/VS 1.4.1
1979	CICS/OS/VS 1.5.0 CICS/DOS/VS 1.5.0
1982	CICS OS/VS 1.6.0
1983	CICS/DOS/VS 1.6.0 CICS/OS/VS 1.6.1
1985	CICS/OS/VS 1.7.0
1986	CICS/DOS/VS 1.7.0
1987	CICS/MVS 2.1.0

Figure 1-1   CICS chronology.

Surprisingly it worked — not at first, but later when it had ma-
tured and after the introduction of virtual storage had put paid to
the hopes and aspirations of rival products such as SHADOW, EN-
VIRON, TASKMASTER, IDMS/DC, etc. From shaky beginnings,

CICS has emerged over the years to become one of IBM's biggest software money spinners (see Figure 1-1 for a CICS chronology).

It is estimated that today there are close to 30,000 licensees of the product all around the world, and, what's more, the figure is increasing and shows no sign of letting up.

As with any IBM product, praise for it is grudging. It is perceived as a cumbersome piece of software, one that requires a great deal of manipulation by systems programmers for it to be installed and work satisfactorily. The applications programmer who writes CICS transactions must also have additional skills and greater understanding in order to use CICS facilities in a sensible manner.

Universal CICS

It is difficult to find an explanation as to why CICS attracts such an enormous following. Its worldwide user base seems to have very little in common. They can't even agree on how to pronounce its name. In North America it is known as "see eye see ess," while in the UK it is called "kicks." Around Europe you may hear it referred to as "cheeks," "theeks," or even "seeks."

Just as varied are the different sectors of industry and commerce that use it. Widespread use of CICS is to be found among leading financial institutions, the retail trade, manufacturing companies, public utilities, local government, the travel industry, and airlines. Peculiar to North America seems to be the use of CICS in hospital and university administration.

Where CICS is strong is in its blueness. It is the sense of stability and security that surrounds it that enables the data processing manager to sleep soundly at night. In addition, the strategic importance that IBM has placed upon CICS has inspired a plethora of software from third-party software vendors. By using CICS to provide the on-line facilities for their products, they have further fueled the continued growth of the product over the years.

Another important contributing factor to its success is the ability of CICS applications to be run with very little or no change under MVS or VSE. Users see this as an ideal path for future growth and protection against any possible loss of value in their software investment.

The Aims of This Book

This book aims at unraveling some of the mysteries behind CICS performance and suggests ways of making improvements through tuning. It is intended to be read by the newcomer and experienced hand alike, and in providing this capability one major concession has had to be made.

To give this book the degree of readability concomitant with it being an effective tool, it has been necessary to reduce the coverage of certain aspects of CICS performance. To give them the amount of analysis they would attract in other books would, in my mind, detract from the importance of the areas that are absolutely crucial and key to achieving efficient CICS systems.

The 80/20 Rule

An experience from my precomputer days has inspired this action and I would like to share it with you. I had just begun the final year of a three-year history course when my teacher, affectionately known as Trog, announced to the class that he was giving up trying to teach us the subject and would instead teach us how to pass the examination at the end of the course. By distilling the syllabus, which covered a period of some 200 years, down to 12 major subjects, we could skip over huge areas of history. He had studied the examination papers for the previous years and had concluded that to pass the examination all we had to do was concentrate our studies on these 12 subjects.

This was my first introduction to a law that I don't think has a name (perhaps I can get it registered as Piggott's Law), but which has appeared with amazing regularity ever since. It is a law which states that 80% of any commodity is made up of 20% of its constituent components.

For example, 80% of the wealth of the world is in the hands of 20% of the population, 20% of all known elements make up 80% of the universe, 80% of IBM's revenues come from 20% of its accounts, and so on. Having duly passed the history examination, perhaps not with flying colors but a pass just the same, I made a mental note to apply this law whenever possible.

I have, as a result, dedicated a large part of my life to obtaining the optimum effect with the minimum of effort. Applied to my work with computer technology, this has paid handsome dividends. Although born out of the laziness of an idle adolescent, it has proved to be a legitimate business tool.

It is a principle that I have applied to the writing of this book and I have therefore tried to concentrate on the 20% or so of tuning areas and techniques available to a CICS Systems Programmer which represent roughly 80% of the sum total of resources consumed by a typical CICS system. By focusing attention on a small subset of CICS facilities, a major tuning exercise can be undertaken without broaching another important law — the law of diminishing returns.

It is quite uncanny how, in most CICS systems, you will find 20% of the total number of files accounting for 80% of all file I/Os, 20% of all communications lines dealing with 80% of all line traffic, and 80% of the CPU time being eaten up by just 20% of the CICS applications.

The Changing Role of the Systems Programmer

When IBM first introduced CICS, it was enough that computing had been transferred to the office from the computer room. A terminal response time of many seconds was quite acceptable. Anything was better than waiting for a batch job to run. Besides, if you had nothing to compare your response time with and you didn't know any better, you could be forgiven for thinking that all was well with the world and that everything in the garden was rosy.

However, it wasn't too long before these early on-line applications gained wider acceptance and more importance. The terminal operators too became more accomplished, and this in turn led to a bigger demand for computer resources.

I first installed CICS in 1979 on a 370/115 running DOS/VS. The network comprised a dozen locally attached display screens, and if I wanted to interrupt the service to the users to apply some maintenance, for example, I simply telephoned the five supervisors and negotiated a convenient time.

Six years later, the same installation was running five CICS systems on two CPUs, one under VSE and the other under MVS. Instead of being a big fish in a small pond, I now found myself a very small fish in an ever-increasing pond. There were hundreds of terminals, remote lines to all parts of the United Kingdom, and plans to link up with the parent company in West Germany and computers all over the world. It now took the equivalent of an Act of Parliament to get any sort of "hands-on" testing.

Our early solutions to CICS performance problems were concerned with channeling extra resources to meet any growing demand for speedier response times, with very little regard for the root cause of the problem. Many of the early CICS systems programmers were more than content just to throw another log on the fire with scant regard for underlying trends and future needs.

In the world of data processing today, and, although I don't have a crystal ball, I suspect even more so tomorrow, this is no longer an acceptable method of dealing with bad performance. Costs were incurred that could easily have been avoided with a more thorough investigation of the problem and a better understanding of its cause.

A far greater reliance is placed on computer systems now than ever in the past, and these systems represent a much higher percentage of the expenditure of most companies. An efficient, well-oiled CICS system can contribute a great deal to the overall profitability of an organization.

By ensuring that the resources at his or her disposal are utilized optimally, the CICS systems programmer can play a big part in ensuring that the company's financial well-being is maintained; it will also do a great deal for his or her confidence and personal marketability.

2

The CICS Environment

This chapter looks at the basic structure of CICS, breaking down its functions into six main areas. It goes on to discuss CICS system generation and concludes by examining some of the performance aspects concerning CICS and the MVS, VSE, and VM operating systems.

Basic CICS Structure

Logically, CICS can be considered as a number of functions which combine to provide six major facilities. Many of these functions constitute the bulk of the CICS nucleus. The six major facilities are:

- System Management
- System Reliability
- System Monitoring
- System Services
- Application Services
- System Support

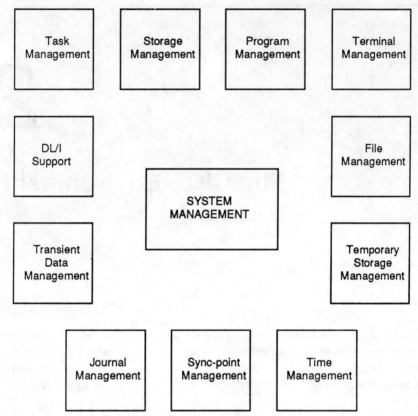

Figure 2-1   System management functions.

System Management

The system management functions (shown in Figure 2-1) are vital to CICS, providing the main driving force performing task control and handling data. System management also provides the interfaces to the operating system and to the various terminal and file access methods.

System Reliability

The system reliability functions (shown on Figure 2-2) provide the mechanisms necessary to deal with any abnormal operating situa-

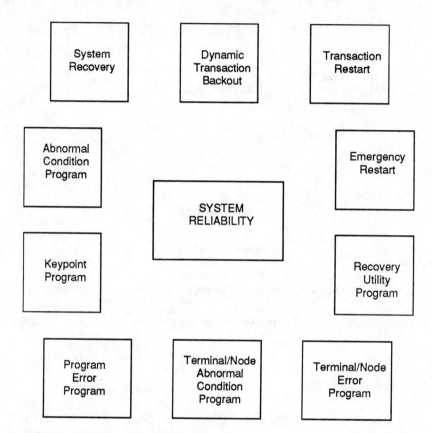

Figure 2-2   System reliability functions.

tions that might occur and to handle system recovery. Installations
can code their own Program Error Program (DFHPEP) to supplement standard CICS error processing.

System Monitoring

The system monitoring functions (shown in Figure 2-3) handle the
collection of statistical and diagnostic data recorded during CICS
operation. This data can be processed with IBM-supplied or user-
written utilities to provide information to help debug applications, to

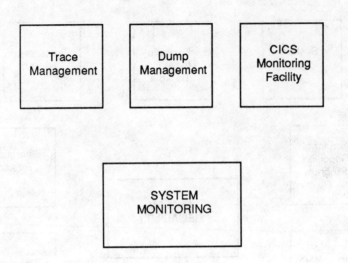

Figure 2-3   System monitoring functions.

investigate CICS performance, or to supply job accounting information.

System Services

The system services functions (shown in Figure 2-4) are sets of modules which form transactions used in the day to day running of CICS. These functions can be used to control access to CICS resources, to monitor and modify the status of CICS resources, to record CICS statistics, and to route messages between terminals.

Application Services

The application services functions (shown in Figure 2-5) add an extra degree of flexibility and usability to user-written applications by providing an interface to system management functions. As a result, the applications programmer is not required to have detailed knowledge of terminal device characteristics as might have otherwise been the case.

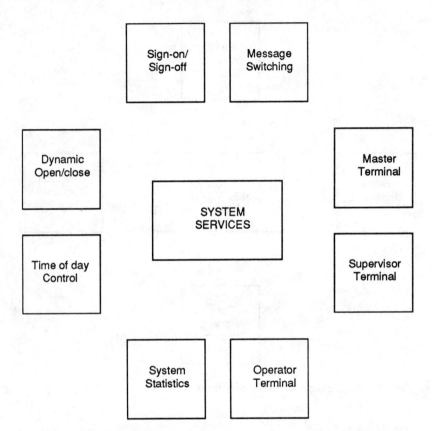

Figure 2-4   System services functions.

System Support

System support functions (shown in Figure 2-6) are mainly off-line utilities that supplement the other functions. Also included in this group of functions are the CICS initialization and termination routines.

CICS System Generation

IBM has progressively, with each successive release of CICS, tried to standardize and simplify the CICS system generation process. This has found a great deal of support among its users but has led to the

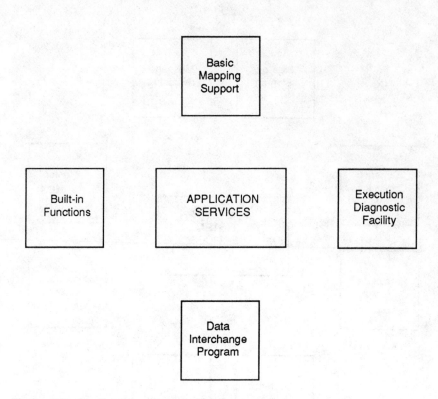

Figure 2-5   Application services functions.

systems programmer having fewer opportunities to cut the size of some of the CICS modules.

With release 1.7 of CICS, the situation is that many modules are now supplied by IBM as either full-function modules or dummy versions — there is no longer anything in between. For example, adding TCAM support, specifying whether the journal control program is to make log records spill on to main or auxiliary storage if the dynamic buffer is full, and activating the High Performance Option (HPO) are all controlled by options in the SIT.

All the other CICS control programs and management modules, with the exception of the Terminal Control Program (TCP), now have a pregenerated version suitable for any combination of selectable options.

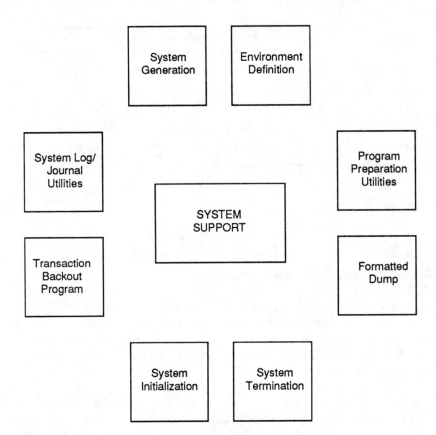

Figure 2-6   System support functions.

Optional CICS Management Modules

The following is a list of some of the CICS management modules with a description of their function, an indication of whether they might be dispensed with altogether, or ideas on how to prevent more functionality being provided than is absolutely necessary. Making sure that CICS is as lean as possible will help to ease the burden on both real and virtual storage.

Basic Mapping Support (BMS). BMS greatly simplifies the interaction between a CICS application and its associated terminal. It offers a degree of device independence to the applications programmer, and

VERSION		
MINIMUM	STANDARD	FULL

	MINIMUM	STANDARD	FULL
COMMAND/ MACRO LEVEL?	Command-level only	Both	Both
FUNCTIONS PROVIDED	SEND MAP RECEIVE MAP SEND CONTROL Default/alternative screens Extended attributes Map set suffixes Screen co-ordination with null maps Block data	As MINIMUM plus: Outboard formats Partitions Controlling magnetic slot reader NLEOM for 3270 system printers SEND TEXT Subsystem LDC controls	As STANDARD plus: Terminal operator paging Cumulative mapping Page overflow Cumulative text processing Message routing Message switching Returning BMS--generated data streams to program before output
DEVICES SUPPORTED	All 3270 terminals except SCS printers	All BMS-supported devices	All BMS-supported devices

Figure 2-7   Comparative BMS options.

its use is widespread. There are three versions available — minimum function, standard function, and full function. The scope of each of these versions is shown in Figure 2-7. Code BMS=MINIMUM STANDARD or FULL in the SIT to select the version appropriate to your installation's needs.

The Built-In Function Program (BFP). The BFP provides support for certain programming functions such as phonetic conversion, data editing, ensuring a data field is alphabetic or numeric, etc., plus support for the weighted retrieval of VSAM data sets. The use of these functions is not widespread and most installations can code BFP=NO in the SIT and not generate support for them.

The CICS Monitoring Program (CMP). The CMP provides a performance data collection facility in addition to standard CICS facilities. Collecting this information at the most detailed level will impose a processing overhead on the system of up to 15%. CMP can be omitted from the system by coding CMP=NO in the SIT.

MCT=NO

The Dynamic Transaction Backout Program (DBP). The DBP ensures that data sets and data bases are restored to their previous state should a transaction abend occur. Obviously, installations that only run on-line enquiry systems would not require this facility. Pregenerated versions with and without DL/I support are provided by IBM — you may select the version appropriate to your site's needs.

The Inter-System Communication Group (ISC). This is actually a number of modules which provide support for sites running the Multi-Region Operation (MRO) or Inter-System Communication (ISC) facilities. Code ISC=NO in the SIT if you do not require this support.

The Journal Control Program (JCP). The JCP is necessary if you are using journaling facilities to record changes to your CICS files, you want support for emergency restarts, you want support for DTB, or you have DL/I data bases. Code JCT=NO in the SIT if you do not use any of these services.

The Terminal Control Program (TCP). The TCP in its fullest version will provide support for every device that could communicate with CICS and for both VTAM and BTAM support. In addition IBM supplies pregenerated versions of the TCP which provide considerably less support (shown in Figure 2-8). If any of these versions are unsuitable, you can generate your own TCP by using the DFHSG PROGRAM=TCP and provide support only for the devices and facilities that you actually need.

DFHTCPA$	SAM support for all devices BTAM support for local 3270 devices
DFHTCPB$	SAM support for all devices BTAM support for local and remote 3270 devices and 3275 dial-up
DFHTCPE$	SAM support for all devices VTAM support for 3270, 3600, and 3790 devices
DFHTCPS$	Full support for all CICS-supported devices and access methods

Figure 2-8 Pre-generated terminal control programs (CICS/OS/VS 1.7).

MVS Considerations

Before starting a CICS performance exercise, you must ensure that MVS has been tuned first and that it is running to its fullest capabilities. You cannot expect to extract the optimum performance from your CICS system if the operating system under which it is running is not functioning at its very best. Make sure that you have a full appreciation of the MVS workload and the overall operational objectives of the computer center.

CICS and the Rest of the Workload

If CICS is running on a dedicated CPU, or perhaps with just a few batch jobs, there is no real problem. If, on the other hand, CICS has to share the resources of MVS with, say, a large TSO population, or with a production IMS/DC system, or if you have more than one CICS system running together on one CPU, then you must tread carefully to avoid worsening the performance of these other subsystems while improving the performance of the CICS system that you are tuning. Most improvements to the CICS system will be at the expense of other jobs. Take care not to degrade their performance unless you have clear authority to do so.

CICS Paging Under MVS

CICS paging is an asynchronous task that causes the entire region to wait for its completion. However, there are some actions peculiar to MVS systems, that can be taken in order to lessen its impact.

For optimum performance, CICS should be defined as nonswappable in the MVS Program Properties Table. Another important consideration that will negate many of the adverse effects experienced in high paging environments is to use real storage isolation or "fencing," as it is also known. This involves defining maximum and minimum values in the Performance Working Set Size (PWSS) parameter of the IEAIPSxx member of SYS1.PARMLIB. These values represent the minimum and maximum number of Real Storage Frames (RSF) required to maintain performance and should be calculated, using

```
WKL=(1,50,99,100)              /* WORKLOAD LEVEL */
OBJ=1,SRV=(1000)               /* TOP PRIORITY */
     .
     .
DMN=5,CNSTR+(5,10)             /* CICS */
     .
     .
PGN=10,(DMN=5,DP=F33,OBJ=1,PWSS=(400,800)) /* CICS */
     .
     .
```

If CICS requires 600 Real Storage Frames (RSFs) to support
normal processing (ie not at peak loading), then the maximum
and minimum Page Working Set Size (PWSS) boundaries should be
set at minus and plus one third of this figure ie PWSS=(400,800).

Figure 2-9   Coding the IEAIPS member for CICS usage.

RMFMON or something similar, from the number of RSFs used by
CICS during normal operation. Figure 2-9 shows how this might be
implemented.

CICS Priority Under MVS

When defining the performance groups in your MVS system, careful
consideration must be given to the order of priority for CICS. For
best performance results, CICS should be given a priority just below
that of VTAM. It should be obvious that any jobs or subsystems
placed above CICS will adversely affect its performance.

While we are on the subject of MVS performance groups, I have
observed many installations where some personnel have, with varying degrees of freedom and control, been given the ability to use the
MVS RESET command. I have seen this command used in an almost
cavalier fashion to reset the performance groups of urgent batch
reruns to those normally reserved for CICS, JES, VTAM, etc. Such
actions can often cause more performance problems than they solve,
especially if it becomes common practice and the operations staff become blasé about its use. Education is the answer. Make sure that
operators are always aware of the impact that their actions can
have.

CICS as an MVS Started Task

It is possible to make a small saving of at least 76K of LSQA by having CICS run as a started task instead of executing it as a long running batch job. This will also reduce the amount of fragmentation of the area of storage located above your specified region size. This area is used by LSQA, SWA, and the 229 and 230 subpools, as shown in Figure 2-10.

Exploiting Virtual I/O Under CICS

You might want to consider copying the contents of your CICS library to a Virtual Input/Output (VIO) data set prior to CICS initialization. By taking advantage of the more efficient I/O routines used by VIO, the average response times of users can be reduced quite dramatically. New copies of programs can be catered for by creating an empty CICS library and putting it before your VIO file in the DFHRPL concatenation. This concept has even greater sig-

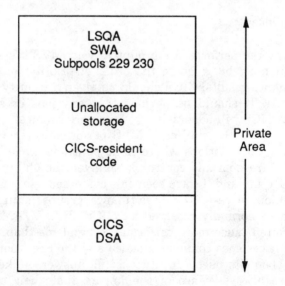

Figure 2-10   CICS storage under MVS.

nificance for those running CPUs in the IBM 3090 series with IBM's announcement in October 1987 of support for VIO in Expanded Storage. Figure 2-11 illustrates the process.

VSE Considerations

As with MVS, it is impossible to achieve maximum performance from a badly implemented or incorrectly defined operating system. While it is true that VSE is a simpler operating system, there is still a fair amount of judgment and understanding required on the part of the VSE systems programmer to ensure that, for example, sufficient copy blocks and channel queue entries are generated while restricting support for the number of partitions and VSE tasks to realistic levels. Although the mechanisms for controlling performance are cruder and less flexible than the MVS or VM equivalents, there is still some scope for ensuring that adequate resources are channeled towards CICS.

```
//STEP1      EXEC PGM=IEBCOPY
//SYSPRINT   DD   SYSOUT=A
//SYSUT1     DD
//SYSUT2     DD
//SYSUT3     DD
//SYSUT4     DD
//OUT        DD   DSN=&&TEMP,DISP=(NEW,PASS),UNIT=VIO,
//                SPACE=(CYL,(..,..,..)),DCB=BLKSIZE=...
//IN         DD   DSN=cics.user.library,DISP=SHR
//SYSIN      DD   *
 C I=IN,O=OUT
/*
//STEP2      EXEC PGM=IEFBR14
//CICSLIB    DD   DSN=cics.newcopy.library,DISP=(NEW,CATLG),
//                VOL=SER=xxxxxx,SPACE=(CYL,(..,,..),
//                DCB=BLKSIZE=.....,UNIT=SYSDA
//STEP3      EXEC PGM=DFHSIP
//DFHRPL     DD   DSN=cics.newcopy.library,DISP=(SHR,DELETE)
//           DD   DSN=&&TEMP,DISP=(OLD,DELETE)
//           DD   other CICS libraries
```

Figure 2-11   Using VIO for the CICS program library.

The PRTY Command

The VSE PRTY command is used to set the priorities of the partitions. The recommended order (in ascending order of importance) is VSE/POWER, VTAM (if present), CICS partition(s), batch partitions. If you are running more than one CICS system, they can be given equal priorities if appropriate. As with the MVS RESET command, I have seen the PRTY command used with an almost reckless regard for its consequences. Many conscientious system operators let themselves get carried away in trying to get batch work run as quickly as possible. Although their actions are well intentioned, they should be made fully aware of the effect that raising the priority of batch partitions above that of CICS has on the response times of the CICS users. Figure 2-12 illustrates a typical VSE system, while Figure 2-13 shows how a typical VSE partition is subdivided under CICS.

The TPBAL Command

The TPBAL command, despite its dubious parentage (it was once only available as an unsupported add-on facility from IBM Systems Engineers), is now a respectable and useful VSE operator command. It stands for Teleprocessing Balancing and determines the number of partitions for which VSE will suspend processing should performance drop because of excessive paging.

For example, if you are running two batch partitions and you enter TPBAL 2, VSE should respond with the partition-ids of your two batch partitions. If this is not the case, you have not specified the PRTY order correctly or it has been changed — this could well be the cause of your problems. This means that if the VSE scheduler determines that paging is too high, the two batch partitions will be temporarily suspended from processing until the situation clears. Other partitions will continue to process normally.

CICS and VSE/POWER

Many installations have applications, either written by themselves or by third party software vendors, that communicate interactively with

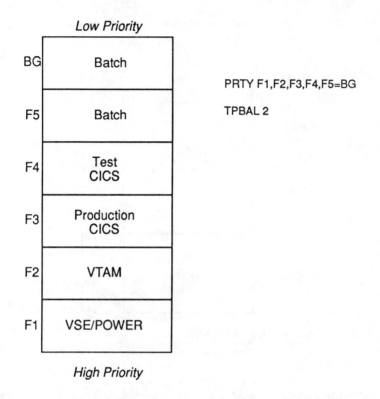

Figure 2-12   A typical VSE system.

the spool files held by VSE/POWER. They interface with VSE/POWER via the PUTSPOOL, GETSPOOL, and CTLSPOOL macros. Unfortunately, in each of these macros there is coded a VSE XWAIT macro, which when invoked causes the whole VSE partition to wait. Using the newer VSE/POWER XPCCB macros prevents this problem.

Special Applications

CICS under VSE has become a convenient vehicle for many different types of terminal-based applications. As many VSE shops run

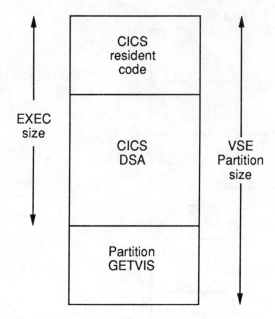

Figure 2-13 CICS storage under VSE.

BTAM, this makes a lot of sense. BTAM does not have the multiap-
plication facilities of VTAM, and so it is necessary for CICS to provide an interface to applications which are otherwise stand-alone. In
this category are IBM's Interactive Command Control Facility
(ICCF) and Applied Data Research's ADR/VOLLIE. Both of these
contain a great deal of potential to hog resources. Therefore, their
performance problems become the performance problems of CICS.

I am not advocating that you not use these products; quite the
contrary, they are both excellent products. Just be aware of the adverse effects that they can have on your CICS system.

In ICCF, interactive compiles, or indeed any of the pseudo-parti-
tion facilities should be avoided at all costs. Both ADR/VOLLIE and
ICCF have powerful procedure languages which can be used to good
effect. Unfortunately they only produce interpretive code and are
consequently very slow when executing. Neither is suited to anything
other than trivial tasks.

VM Considerations

When configuring a VM environment, it is essential that no single virtual machine has an unintended influence on the performance of other virtual machines executing at the same time. The Control Program's (CP) scheduler uses an algorithm based on the virtual machine's user priority, the amount of elapsed time since the virtual machine was last dispatched, the amount of CPU time used by the virtual machine, and the overall load on the machine to determine which virtual machine to dispatch next. It is important to bear these factors in mind when adjusting any of the following CP options which greatly affect CICS in particular in the VM environment.

The Priority Option

The PRIORITY option can be used to assign a priority value to a virtual machine. The priority value can be any figure in the range 1 to 99 (the lower the value, the higher the priority). Because of the nature of CP's scheduling (see above), the virtual machine with the highest user priority may not necessarily be the first to be dispatched.

The Favor Option

The FAVOR option can be used to control the rate at which a virtual machine is allowed to use the available CPU time. The option has two basic forms. In the form CP SET FAVORED *user*, CP keeps the virtual machine *user* permanently in its run list, which is its list of currently dispatchable virtual machines. In the form CP SET FAVORED *user nnn*, CP will allow the virtual machine *user* to use *nnn*% of the available CPU time. If *nnn* is set at 100, CP will always attempt to dispatch that virtual machine first.

The Lock Option

The LOCK option can be used to maintain certain virtual storage pages in real storage. These pages will be taken from the common page pool, which will obviously affect all virtual machines. The pages locked into real storage must be explicitly referenced by their virtual addresses. Since these locations are prone to fluctuation, the LOCK option will probably prove to be impractical at most VM sites.

The Reserve Option

The RESERVE option can be used to define a number of real storage page frames which are to be reserved for the exclusive use of a specific virtual machine. This option provides a lot more flexibility than the LOCK option. Pages can be paged out but only by pages belonging to the same virtual machine.

The QDROP OFF Option

The QDROP OFF option can be used to exclude pages for a virtual machine from the flush list. The flush list is a list of pages of an inactive virtual machine that can be flushed from the system when the VM systems resources manager determines that the paging rate is too high. This is a particularly useful option in low-activity CICS systems under VM, as it prevents them from being paged out during periods of CICS inactivity. High-activity CICS systems under VM can also benefit, but to a lesser degree, as page faults will be reduced because more pages will be in real storage.

3

How CICS Works

It is very important that anyone who is going to attempt to tune a CICS system or investigate its potential for performance improvements first has at the very least, a basic knowledge of the CICS mechanisms described in this chapter. A fundamental appreciation of the internal workings of CICS and some idea of how the various components interact are prerequisites for the would-be tuner.

CICS Interfaces

A casual observer might be forgiven for thinking that the OS and DOS versions of CICS were completely unrelated animals, born of different parents. This is the complete opposite of the true story. It has always been IBM's policy to keep the two products as similar as possible and to restrict any differences in the code of the two products to an absolute minimum.

To achieve this admirable goal, the developers of CICS have had to write code to perform many tasks normally carried out by the operating system or one of its subsystems. In particular, in order for CICS/OS and CICS/DOS to appear indistinguishable, CICS has its own routines to handle file management, terminal management, and storage management.

Where CICS needs to trade information with one of IBM's principal access methods (either a file access method or a terminal access method), it does so via an approved interface. The best known of these interfaces are the VSAM interface, the DL/I interface, and the VTAM interface. The most important interface is the interface with the operating system itself.

Task Management

CICS is a multitasking system, which means that several tasks can be processed concurrently. As tasks enter the system, they are assigned a priority. This priority is a numeric value between 0 and 255 and is the sum of the values defined in the TRNPRTY parameter of the PCT, the OPPRTY parameter of the SNT, and the TRMPRTY parameter of the TCT, up to a maximum value of 255, as shown in Figure 3-1.

Trying to assess a priority based on all three of these parameters will prove unmanageable in a CICS system with any degree of complexity at all and will even prove to be hard work if based on just two of the three parameters. It is advisable to concentrate solely on one of the parameters (TRNPRTY will be the most appropriate in the majority of cases) and not to assign a priority of 255 to any transaction except CEMT.

Tasks are placed on the active task queue until the value specified in the AMXT parameter of the SIT is exceeded, i.e., the maximum number of tasks defined for the CICS system has been reached. Each

Table	Parameter	Acceptable values	Default
PCT	TRNPRTY	0-255	1
SNT	OPPRTY	0-255	0
TCT	TRMPRTY	0-255	0

Figure 3-1 Assigning task priorities under CICS.

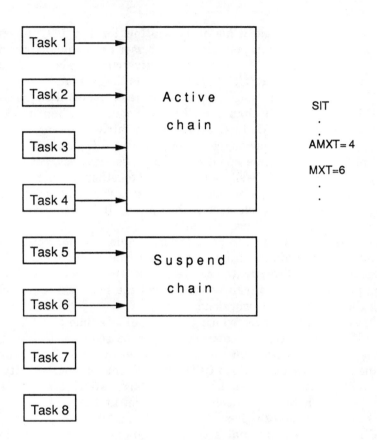

Figure 3-2   Using MXT and AMXT to control task flow.

task will be processed in order of age within priority on a First In, First Out (FIFO) basis, as shown in Figure 3-2.

CICS creates a Dispatch Control Area (DCA) for each task that it accepts for processing. The number of tasks it can accept is governed by the MXT parameter of the SIT. DCAs are chained together on two separate chains, an active chain and a suspended chain. CICS will place on the suspended chain a task for which it does not anticipate receiving a processing request during a relatively long period of time. This could occur while a task is waiting for terminal I/O to complete, for example, but not while it is waiting for file I/O, unless the resource is unavailable because another user has enqueued upon it.

A task is transferred back to the active chain by a CICS control program issuing a RESUME specifying the task's TCA.

Multitasking is accomplished when a task makes a request for a CICS resource other than the CPU, for example, when it needs to perform some file I/O. In CICS, this is a fairly frequent occurrence and, because the time taken to service this I/O is considerable in comparison to the time spent on CPU processing, several tasks are happy to coexist. So well can they run together at many installations, in fact, that the end-user can be forgiven if he or she thinks that he or she is the sole user of the system. It is the absence of this perception that causes user complaints.

Because the initiative to drive the mechanism responsible for CICS multitasking originates from within the requests made for CICS services by the applications themselves, tasks that differ in their execution profile from what can be considered the norm can adversely affect the balance of the workload.

In short, any task for which the ratio of I/O time to CPU time is small has the potential to disrupt the service given to other users. To some extent this problem can be alleviated by giving short-running transactions with a smallish CPU requirement a higher priority than the CPU gluttons and long browsers. Unfortunately, this in itself will not prevent a task monopolizing a system at the expense of other tasks once it has been given control.

One way to ensure that a task relinquishes control from time to time is to add CICS DELAY or SUSPEND requests to portions of code likely to be CPU-intensive.

Another way is to use the TCLASS parameter of the PCT and the CMXT parameter of the SIT to limit the numbers of certain classes of transactions active at any given time to acceptable levels. This latter option should only be considered by CICS 1.7 and above users as the retry logic associated with this mechanism for previous releases of CICS had the potential to create loops in addition to being a high user of CPU time. This has been greatly changed in release 1.7 and should no longer be a consideration.

Making use of either or both of these facilities may still not be sufficient to completely rid you of the problem of certain transactions hogging your system. These resource hogs will be passed control, in preference to any tasks of equal priority, as soon as the task to which they have handed control needs any sort of CICS service.

To avoid this situation you could consider extending the logic of the task dispatcher so that the servicing of all active tasks is performed on a fairer basis.

This is by no means a trivial task but it can be done by rewriting or modifying the Task Control Program, DFHKCP, although a much simpler method (and one that should have the approval of IBM) would be to write a user exit routine which would get control prior to the dispatching of a task. The particular exit introduced for such a purpose is called XKCDISP.

By introducing logic to place a task at the bottom of the queue of tasks of equal priority waiting to be dispatched, the age of a task plays no part in a task's dispatchability. In this way, the queue is processed on a rotational basis and not on a FIFO basis.

This has the overall effect of allowing CICS to process short-running tasks faster than long-running tasks of equal priority. Under normal circumstances, this means that overall throughput is improved and the response times of short-running tasks are reduced at the expense of longer response times for long-running tasks.

The big danger in coding this user exit, or any other user exit, is if it becomes too elaborate and increases the overall CPU time for CICS. After all, in the case of the XKCDISP exit, every single task will invoke this exit. Make sure that once addressability has been established, the first thing you do is check that the routine is applicable.

For instance, if we take the above example, the first thing we should do is make sure that we are not dealing with a CICS management task. These tasks have alphabetic rather than numeric task identifiers and so the first thing to do is to check the task number, which is contained in the TCAKCTTA field of the TCA. If it is not numeric we should exit at once.

Similarly, we do not want to interfere with any tasks that have a priority of 255. By checking the TCTTEOP (operator priority) field of the TCTTE, the TCTTETP (terminal priority) field of the TCTTE, and the TCATCDP (transaction priority) field of the TCA, we can determine if we need proceed any further.

CICS task management does seem to work fairly well in practice, although it is not an ideal mechanism. It is good to know the types of transaction that can have an adverse or disproportionate effect on the CICS workload and what measures can be taken to negate their influence on other transactions.

Storage Management

A CICS partition or region contains three distinct areas:

• CICS resident code
• Partition GETVIS (VSE) or OSCOR (MVS)
• CICS Dynamic Storage Area (DSA)

It is the DSA that is of most interest to us in this chapter.

The DSA is controlled by the Storage Control Program (DFHSCP), which uses the Page Allocation Map (PAM) to keep track of which areas of Dynamic Storage it has allocated to which tasks.

CICS tries to predict the manner in which various facilities will utilize the DSA and to this end it divides the DSA into seven separate subpools, which are numbered from one to eight (subpool seven is conspicuous by its absence). Each subpool handles storage allocation and control in slightly different ways. The seven subpools are:

• Control subpool
• Teleprocessing subpool
• Mixed subpool
• Isolated subpool
• Shared subpool
• RPL subpool
• Program subpool

Control Subpool

The control subpool is used to hold some small but important CICS control blocks. Among these are the Dispatch Control Area (DCA), the Queue Element Area (QEA), the Interval Control Element (ICE), and the Automatic Initiate Descriptor (AID).

Teleprocessing Subpool

The teleprocessing subpool is used to hold the I/O areas used by the terminal and the line. The most common I/O areas that will be encountered are Terminal Input Output Area (TIOA), Receive Any Input Area (RAIA), and Line Input Output Area (LIOA).

Mixed Subpool

The mixed subpool is used to hold the task-related storage of transactions defined in the PCT as CLASS=SHORT. CLASS=SHORT is not supported for transactions defined using RDO, and it is reasonably safe to ignore the option altogether on macro-defined tables.

Isolated Subpool

The isolated subpool is used to hold the task-related storage of transactions defined in the PCT as CLASS=LONG. The significant control blocks include the Task Control Area (TCA), the Register Storage Area (RSA), the Journal Control Area (JCA), and areas for temporary storage, transient data, and files.

Shared Subpool

The shared subpool is used to hold common work areas which are not associated with any task in particular but which can be used by any tasks. Under this heading comes temporary storage; the COMMAREA; BMS maps; and the DL/I control blocks, the Data Management Blocks (DMBs), the Program Specification Blocks (PSBs), and the Enqueue (ENQ) blocks.

Request Parameter List (RPL) Subpool

The RPL subpool is used to hold the RPLs required by VTAM terminal management. This subpool is usually quite small in comparison with the others.

Program Subpool

The program subpool is used to hold nonresident application programs and maps. The program subpool is allocated from the top of the DSA downward, and each program and map is positioned on a page boundary.

Virtual Storage Constraint

The very essence of virtual storage has been, since its inception, the ability to overcommit real storage. This enables programs to be run which are considerably larger than the real storage available to them.

Under CICS, virtual storage is overcommitted in the standard way by being executed in a partition or region which is larger than the amount of real storage allocated to it. In the average CICS system, virtual storage is also overcommitted in the DSA, where we typically have the situation where the amount of virtual storage allocated to the DSA is only a fraction of what could be required should the worst possible mix of concurrent transactions occur.

We have already seen that the DSA is set out with the program subpool at the top and the remaining subpools at the bottom. The pages used by the program subpool are not released automatically once they have been finished with. This means that any action CICS takes to clean up the program subpool occurs only when there is an urgent need for it to do so.

Program Compression

If you are fortunate enough to have one of the more expensive performance monitors running on your CICS system, you may well have seen a graphic display of the DSA and its subpools — a display in which the program subpool at the top of the DSA and the remaining subpools at the bottom gradually (I hope) inch nearer and nearer to each other until they merge and then retire to their original positions, only to repeat the process all over again.

This graphical representation, although pleasing to the eye and reminiscent of some sort of arcade game, is actually showing you a program compression taking place. It is much better to witness it taking place on someone else's system.

A program compression occurs in a CICS system which is said to be "under stress." This rather dramatic expression refers to a situation in which CICS is unable to satisfy a GETMAIN request from the DSA because it has insufficient virtual storage available to it.

Program compressions impart considerable overhead when they take place. Not only are they highly CPU-intensive, but they also bring about an increase in paging.

All nonresident programs that are no longer in use are purged from the program subpool. Flags are set (PAMDELET) for the remaining programs in the Page Allocation Map (PAM) so that when they are finished with, they will also be purged. A small number of program compressions are, of course, inevitable.

Going "Short-on-Storage"

In most circumstances, the cleaning up of DSA which occurs with a program compression will be sufficient for the GETMAIN that brought it about to be satisfied. In the event of CICS still being unable to meet the GETMAIN requirement, a "short-on-storage" situation is recorded.

In this situation, an area of the DSA set aside for use in such an emergency and called the storage cushion is used. The size of the storage cushion is defined by the SCS parameter of the SIT, or it can be altered dynamically by using the CEMT SET CUS(value) command.

While it is "short-on-storage," CICS will not accept any new tasks into the system and will stop polling CICS terminals.

System Stress

If the use of the storage cushion still fails to realize enough virtual storage, things are really getting pretty serious. The system is now in what is called a state of "system stress," but all is not lost as CICS still has a couple of tricks up its sleeve.

The AMXT value, which is defined in the SIT, is temporarily set to 999 to allow, if possible, tasks to finish processing and to be purged from the system.

If this doesn't work, CICS will wait for the length of time defined in the ICVS parameter of the SIT. This period of time is called the stall purge interval. CICS will then abend any tasks which have been defined as "stall purgeable" (i.e., they have been defined in the PCT as SPURGE=YES).

This is the absolute last resort. In the event of there still not being enough virtual storage available to meet the GETMAIN, there is nothing else that can be done. CICS will have to be cancelled and restarted.

All of the above actions are extremely costly in terms of CPU consumption and paging. In practice, in systems with extremely inadequate DSAs, CICS tends to limp about in agony for several minutes, sometimes hours, after experiencing its first "short-on-storage" condition before succumbing totally and accepting its inevitable fate. During this time, users will experience erratic response at their terminals. As this response time gets more and more unpredictable, their tempers will become more and more frayed.

4

Choosing CICS Parameters

This chapter takes a look at the CICS tables and discusses the considerations that should be made when selecting values and settings for parameters that have a bearing on CICS performance.

Introduction

There can very little doubt that accepting the default values for any of the numerous parameters applicable to any of the CICS tables without assessing their possible impact will leave you with a very inefficient system. Choosing an appropriate value is not a simple matter, however, and great care must be exercised to avoid ending up with an unhealthy CICS.

As always, you have to make some sort of a trade-off when considering what is best for your particular installation, and you will have to weigh the pros and cons for each individual circumstance. In most cases there is no answer that is always going to be the right one. In some cases the selection of an appropriate value will have far greater importance and a much larger impact on performance than others. There will be occasions when you can get away with a wrong choice, while poor judgment elsewhere could bring your CICS system to a grinding halt.

This chapter looks at the CICS tables and highlights the important parameters from the view of improving performance.

The Application Load Table (ALT)

The majority of installations don't have an ALT and I see no reason to question their judgment. You can safely live without it and I think that most installations see it as having limited value.

It is used basically to change the order in which resident programs are loaded at CICS start-up time. If it is not specified, resident programs are loaded in the order in which they appear in the PPT. It can be used effectively to control the way in which virtual storage is allocated for resident programs and to group-related programs in order to minimize paging. Some sites use it in order to keep programs and their related maps together in real storage.

There is a danger of coding it for optimum use but then forgetting about it, with the result that subsequent changes and additions to the system negate its effectiveness.

ADRSPCE=HIGH|LOW

This parameter is used to specify whether the program is to be loaded from the top or from the bottom of the storage area used for resident programs and can be used to separate programs into two distinct groups.

ALIGN=NO|ENTRY|YES

This parameter is used to specify whether a program is to be aligned on a page boundary or packed together with others. If specified as YES, those loaded in the low address space will begin on a page boundary, while those loaded in the high address space will end on a page boundary. The ENTRY keyword can be specified for programs in the low address space to ensure that the entry point to a program is on a page boundary and that the unreferenced part of the program, typically consisting of an eyecatcher, timestamp and datestamp information, will be on the previous page.

FIX=NO|YES

This parameter will let a program have its pages fixed in real storage. In my experience, it is much better to let the operating system use its own routines to control paging, and I do not recommend its use.

PAGEOUT=NO|YES

This parameter will force the program out of real storage when it is not being used. Again, I would not use it for the same reasons that I would not use FIX=YES in the ALT.

The Destination Control Table (DCT)

The DCT contains the entries for transient data queues. There are two types of transient data: intra-partition transient data which, as its name suggests, is administered internally by CICS and placed in a "catch all" data set called DFHNTRA, and extra-partition transient data, which is kept on sequential data sets defined by the user.

Intra-partition destinations and extra-partition destinations are defined in the TYPE=INTRA and TYPE=EXTRA macro instructions respectively. Each TYPE=EXTRA macro instruction, has a related TYPE=SDSCI instruction. There is one more type of macro, and that is the TYPE=INDIRECT instruction. This is used to group multiple logical destinations together so they appear as just one physical destination.

OPEN=INITIAL|DEFERRED

This is a TYPE=EXTRA parameter and can be used to delay the opening of the data set. The DEFERRED opening of data sets will speed up CICS system initialization time slightly.

REUSE=YES|NO

This is a TYPE=INTRA parameter. Only code REUSE=NO if you have written your own program to process the CICS DFHNTRA data set.

BUFNO=1|number

This is a TYPE=SDSCI parameter and is used to specify the number of buffers to be allocated to the related extra-partition data set. Under CICS/DOS any number apart from 2 will default to 1. Under CICS/OS any figure from 1 to 255 can be specified. Code a value to prevent any task waiting for buffers and monitor this value by checking the CICS statistics.

The File Control Table (FCT)

The FCT contains the entries for the data sets processed under CICS. The two macro instructions of primary concern are the TYPE=DATASET and TYPE=SHRCTL macro instructions. The chapter on File Handling addresses many of these parameters in much greater detail, although a summary of the primary considerations is given here for completeness.

With support for ISAM files discontinuing from releases of CICS 1.7 onwards, they are not considered in this section.

BUFND=number (VSAM only)

This is a TYPE=DATASET parameter and it is used to specify the number of VSAM data buffers to be reserved for the use of a data set. The minimum specification is for a value of STRNO (see the STRNO parameter) plus 1. The value is ignored by VSAM for data sets participating in Local Shared Resources (see the SERVREQ= SHR parameter), although CICS uses the value to calculate the amount of virtual storage to be allocated to the Local Shared Resource buffer pool.

BUFNI=number (VSAM only)

This is a TYPE=DATASET parameter and it is used to specify the number of VSAM index buffers to be reserved for the use of a data set. The minimum required by VSAM is STRNO (see the STRNO parameter). For small files it might be possible to hold the entire index in main storage. Ideally, you should try to hold the lowest level of index, the sequence set, in main storage. The value is ignored by VSAM for data sets participating in Local Shared Resources (see the SERVREQ=SHR parameter), although CICS uses the value to calculate the amount of virtual storage to be allocated to the Local Shared Resource buffer pool.

BUFFERS=(size(count),.....)

This is a TYPE=SHRCTL parameter used to override the allocation of buffers for Local Shared Resources, calculated by CICS. The size of the buffers is specified in bytes; they must be powers of 2. The minimum value is 512 bytes and the maximum is 32,768 bytes. At least three buffers must be allocated to each size.

Buffers are allocated on 4K boundaries so there is no point in allocating, for instance, less than eight 512 byte buffers or less than four 1K buffers.

BUFSP=number (VSAM only)

This is a TYPE=DATASET parameter, and it is used to specify in bytes the amount of buffer space to be allocated to a dataset. It is better to concentrate on getting the values for BUFND and BUFNI correct and letting CICS work out for itself an appropriate value.

KEYLEN=number

This is a TYPE=SHRCTL parameter. It is used to specify the maximum key length of any of the data sets using the Local Shared Resources buffer pool. It should be coded if you are not going to accept the default allocations calculated by CICS to prevent accesses to the VSAM catalog, which will occur if it is not defined.

LOG=NO|YES

This is a TYPE=DATASET parameter. Only specify LOG=YES if the file is updated on-line, otherwise unnecessary overhead may be incurred. It might sound obvious, but I have seen installations code LOG=YES for all their files regardless of their on-line function.

RECFORM=([UNDEFINED|VARIABLE|FIXED][BLOCKED|UNBLOCKED])

This is a TYPE=DATASET parameter. The default for VSAM files is VARIABLE,BLOCKED. Mistakenly specifying UNBLOCKED will incur additional overhead.

RSCLMT=number

This is a TYPE=SHRCTL parameter. CICS calculates a maximum size for the Local Shared Resources pool, and RSCLMT specifies what percentage of this calculation is actually to be allocated.

SERVREQ=SHR

This is a TYPE=DATASET parameter. SERVREQ=SHR is used to denote that a particular data set is to share the Local Shared Resources pool and not have its own buffers allocated. Under most circumstances LSR is strongly recommended. The argument for its implementation and exceptions are explained in Chapter 7, Processing CICS Files.

STRNO=1|number (VSAM only)

As a TYPE=DATASET parameter, this is used to specify how many concurrent requests may be processed against a data set up to a maximum of 255. The number of string waits for a data set given in the CICS statistics will enable you to assess the accuracy of the value specified. Waiting on strings is not necessarily a bad thing if it prevents other resources from becoming overcommitted. The value is ignored by VSAM for data sets participating in Local Shared Resources (see the SERVREQ=SHR parameter), although CICS uses the value to calculate the amount of virtual storage to be allocated to the Local Shared Resource buffer pool.

STRNO=number

As a TYPE=SHRCTL parameter, this is used to override the CICS-calculated value for the number of strings to be allocated to data sets using the Local Shared Resources pool. Ideally, it should be set to represent the total number of concurrent users of Local Shared Resources at any given time.

STRNOG=number (VSAM and CICS/OS only)

This is a TYPE=DATASET parameter and is used to specify the number of strings to be used for read only processing. It will default to 20% of the value given for STRNO (see STRNO parameter). Specify a value of 0 if you only ever do READ FOR UPDATE processing on the data set.

The Journal Control Table (JCT)

The JCT contains entries for every journal data set. There are two types of journal data sets: the system log and user journals.

BUFSIZE=number

This is used to specify the size in bytes of the output buffer for journal data sets. The minimum allowed is 72 bytes, unless DL/I logging is to take place when it is 1100 bytes, and the maximum is the track size of the DASD being used for CKD devices, 32,761 bytes for FBA devices, or 32,767 bytes for tape files. Initially set this to the size of the average block that is going to be written to the journal data set multiplied by the number of concurrent tasks using the journal data set. The suitability of this estimate can be gauged by inspecting the CICS statistics.

BUFSUV=number

This is known as the buffer shift up value, and it is a threshold value specified as a number of bytes for starting I/O to the journal data set. Journal data set I/O will start when the amount of data in the journal buffer exceeds this figure. If a value is not specified, CICS will take the BUFSIZE value as a default. Start with a value 75% of BUFSIZE and adjust it accordingly based on CICS statistics.

JTYPE=SMF (CICS/OS only)

This parameter is used to define the type of data set being used to record journal data and is usually TAPEn or DISKn. If you are collecting CMF data, you can write it to the MVS SMF data set, which is more efficient than writing it to a CICS journal data set.

SYSWAIT=STARTIO|ASIS

This specifies how system journaling synchronization requests are to be handled. The *CICS Performance* manual very strongly suggests that you accept the default. If you choose to ignore this advice, be sure you have a good reason.

The Nucleus Load Table (NLT)

The NLT is an optional facility with which you can alter the order in which the CICS nucleus is loaded at system initiation time. The default order should be adequate for all but the most discerning of users, and I would consider the effort in coming up with an alternative load order to be a lot of work for very little reward.

ADRSPCE=LOW|HIGH

This parameter is used to specify at which end of the address space or partition the module is to be loaded. The default for CICS/OS is HIGH, whereas for CICS/DOS it is LOW.

ALIGN=NO|ENTRY|YES

This parameter is used to specify whether a program is to be aligned on a page boundary or packed together with others. If specified as YES, those loaded in the low address space will begin on a page boundary, while those loaded in the high address space will end on a page boundary. The ENTRY keyword can be specified for programs in the low address space to ensure that the entry point to a program is on a page boundary and that the unreferenced part of the program, typically consisting of an eyecatcher, timestamp and datestamp information will be on the previous page.

FIX=NO|YES

Coding FIX=YES allows the module to have its pages fixed in real storage. It is very much a luxury. I, personally, would let the operating system look after paging with its own routines and would not try to intervene. Obviously tuning the paging subsystem at the operating system level will have much more impact than doing it at the application level (I am looking at CICS here as just another application being run under the operating system). Unless you really know what you are doing, you stand as much chance of degrading performance as improving it.

PAGEIN=NO|YES (CICS/DOS only)

Coding PAGEIN=YES will add this module to a special list of modules called the "page-in list." A page-in operation is actioned, based on this list, each time that CICS regains control following a VSE WAIT, which is invoked by KCP. Again, it can be used to preempt the paging routines of the operating system and for the reasons I have already given, I would not advocate its use, except perhaps in a lightly used CICS partition running against a lot of batch processing and maybe other more critical CICS systems.

PAGEOUT=NO|YES (CICS/DOS only)

Page-out operations can be affected in a similar way to page-in operations by specifying PAGEOUT=YES. Entries of modules infrequently used can be included to help reduce the size of the CICS working set.

The Program Control Table (PCT)

The PCT is not so much a Program Control Table as a Transaction Control Table, for it describes a transaction and its characteristics with one entry reserved for the name of the program to be given control whenever that transaction is invoked. It is one of the tables that can be generated using the Resource Definition On-line (RDO) facilities introduced in CICS 1.6.0. RDO limits the system programmer's choice for some parameters — not always to his or her complete satisfaction. For instance, CLASS=LONG, FDUMP= (ASRA,ASRB) and PRIVATE=YES are forced; and the ANTICPG, DTB=NO, and PRMSIZE parameters cannot be specified.

ANTICPG=NO|YES|number (Non-RDO only)

This parameter can be used to specify whether a transaction is to perform anticipatory paging. As its name implies, this means that the transaction will acquire an area of storage at task initialization time for the transaction's Task Control Area (TCA) and data areas. It is another of these parameters that will negate the effectiveness of the operating system's paging algorithms and its use is only recommended for systems that are already paging heavily. If ANTICPG=YES is coded, one page will be initially acquired for the transaction's TCA and data areas. If ANTICPG=number is coded, that number of pages is acquired.

CLASS=LONG|SHORT

This parameter is used to select the storage subpool from which the task's storage is to be allocated. CLASS=LONG will cause the storage to be allocated from the isolated subpool, while

CLASS=SHORT will cause storage to be allocated from the mixed subpool. Using RDO, only CLASS=LONG can be chosen.

Specifying CLASS=SHORT for long-running tasks can cause serious storage fragmentation and increased real storage demands. On the other hand, specifying CLASS=LONG for short-running tasks will probably be unnoticeable. My advice is to take IBM's hint and only code CLASS=LONG.

DTB=NO|YES|(YES,NO)|(YES,WAIT)

This parameter is used to specify whether Dynamic Transaction Backout (DTB) is to be invoked should the transaction terminate abnormally. DTB buffers are only acquired at the time a protected resource is changed, and so incorrectly specifying DTB=YES for an enquiry-only transaction will only incur a minimum overhead.

DTB=(YES,NO) is used in ISC transactions to invoke DTB unless the failure occurs during sync point or program return processing, in which case DTB is not to be invoked. Coding DTB=(YES,WAIT) will cause CICS to lock the protected resources involved until the session has been recovered.

DTIMOUT=NO|number

This parameter is used to specify a deadlock time interval. The value represents the number of minutes and seconds for which CICS will wait should the task become suspended because a resource is not available. When the specified time interval has elapsed, CICS issues an AKCS abend. It can be used to minimize the effects of an existing performance problem. If it must be used, it is better to confine it to enquiry-only transactions. It is better still to pinpoint the reasons for any transaction deadlocks, remove them, and let this default to DTIMOUT=NO.

DUMP=YES|NO

This parameter is used to specify whether a dump is to be produced should the transaction terminate abnormally. Producing a dump will increase CPU contention and real storage. The use of dumps to debug program failures is unique to each installation and depends on, among other things, what other programming debugging tools are available. You may well consider having separate options for production and test running.

FDUMP=(ASRA,ASRB)|ASRA|ASRB

This parameter is used to specify whether a formatted dump is to be produced should the transaction terminate abnormally because of a program interrupt (ASRA) or an operating system abend (ASRB). Similar observations made about the DUMP parameter apply to the FDUMP parameter.

PRMSIZE=number (CICS/OS and non-RDO only)

This parameter is used to specify the number of bytes to be allocated for primed storage for the transaction. Primed storage is allocated at task initiation time and all GETMAINs are satisfied from this area. This has the advantage of speeding up GETMAINs but at the expense of additional virtual and real storage. It is further limited to only transactions defined as CLASS=SHORT. Moreover, in the *CICS Performance* manual, its use is not recommended and current users are urged to plan around its use in the future.

RAQ=NO|YES (VTAM only)

This parameter is used to specify whether SNA protocols are to be maintained for the task or not. If RAQ=YES is specified, read ahead queuing will be done by SNA and incoming data will be queued by CICS on temporary storage. Although it is implied by its name, it is not a performance option. Normally, this parameter is left to default at RAQ=NO.

RESTART=NO|YES

This parameter is used to specify whether the transaction should be restarted in the event of an abend and is usually employed to restart transactions automatically that have entered a "deadly embrace" situation. There is a danger here, unless you take steps to prevent it, of the same transactions being restarted and the same problem recurring indefinitely.

RTIMOUT=NO|number

This parameter is used to specify the amount of time for which a task will wait for input from the terminal. The value represents the number of minutes and seconds for which CICS will wait. When the specified time interval has elapsed, CICS issues an AKCT abend. Many installations that have adopted a pseudo-conversational programming standard use the RTIMOUT parameter to control some of the IBM-supplied conversational transactions, such as CSMT, CEMT, CSSN, etc., which might otherwise be left hanging about by a thoughtless operator. This is the most effective use of the parameter. It can also be used to control MRO/ISC sessions.

SPURGE=NO|YES

This parameter is used to specify whether or not a task is to be purged from the system should it go into a state of "stress." This situation is described in more detail in Chapter 3, How CICS Works. Code SPURGE=YES on read-only transactions that can be purged as a last resort when CICS has entered a "stress" condition.

TCLASS=NO|class number

This parameter is used to specify whether or not a transaction is to be assigned to a particular class or not. The class number is a decimal value from 1 to 10 with no set significance other than that fixed by the installation. The value is used in conjunction with the CMXT parameter of the SIT to limit the number of active transactions of any particular class at any one time. Prior to CICS 1.7, there was a danger of loops occurring when it was used, and as a result it might be overlooked as an effective performance enhancer. Generally, you should group transactions with similar performance profiles together. For example, you could have simple enquiry programs in a class with CMXT set reasonably high, while transactions that hog resources could be assigned to a class with CMXT set to one or two.

TPURGE=NO|YES

This parameter is used to indicate whether a BTAM-attached task can be purged in the event of a terminal error occurring. Don't confuse it with the SPURGE parameter; it's something completely different.

TRACE=YES|NO

This parameter is used to specify whether entries are to be made in the trace table for events connected with this transaction. CICS trace facilities impose a considerable overhead on the system and can be disabled for the whole CICS partition or address space. If you have CICS trace running, you can disable it at the transaction level for reliable programs by coding TRACE=NO.

TRNPRTY=1|number

This parameter is used to assign a priority value to a transaction. The number can be any decimal value between 0 and 255 and it is used in conjunction with priorities assigned at the operator level (see the SNT OPPRTY parameter) and at the terminal level (see the TCT TRMPRTY parameter) to arrive at a value which represents the task's dispatching priority up to a maximum value of 255. Giving different values at all three levels proves unworkable at most installations, and it is advisable that you only use one of the three. Which one you use will depend on your own particular circumstances.

TWASIZE=0|number

This parameter is used to specify the number of bytes to be allocated to the Transaction Work Area (TWA) for this transaction. Any number between 0 and 32,767 can be specified. Specifying too small a value for TWASIZE will result in storage violations, whereas specifying too large a value is wasteful.

The Processing Program Table (PPT)

The PPT contains entries for all programs and maps that are capable of being run on the CICS system. This is another of the tables that can be defined using RDO and the CEDA transaction. All the following recommendations apply to programs or maps defined using RDO, except that USAGE=MAP is not supported and RES can only be defined as YES or NO.

RELOAD=NO|YES

This parameter is used to specify whether a fresh copy of the program is to be loaded every time that a request is issued to load it. RELOAD=YES is mandatory for RPGII programs (CICS/DOS only). Otherwise it has very little to recommend its use.

RES=NO|ALIGN|FIX|PGOUT|YES

This parameter is highly critical to CICS performance. It is used to specify whether a program or map is to be resident in core throughout the entire running of CICS (RES=YES) or whether it should be loaded from the program library (RES=NO).

Program loading under CICS is performed as a serial process, meaning that although other CICS processing can take place at the same time, should another task require the services of the program loader it will have to wait. In a very busy system with a lot of such activity this could prove to be a major bottleneck.

On the other hand, the more programs defined as resident, the bigger the demands on virtual and real storage and the increased likelihood of paging.

RES=YES should be used carefully and ideally for as many of the most heavily used programs and maps as possible without incurring excessive paging overheads.

RES=YES cannot be specified for RPGII programs (CICS/DOS only). ALIGN, FIX, and PGOUT are all variations of RES=YES. Coding RES=YES means that the program is to be made core-resident, but that the operating system can still page it out. RES=ALIGN will align the program on a page boundary. RES=FIX fixes the program's pages and makes them nonpageable. RES=PGOUT will cause CICS to force the program out of real storage when it has finished executing; this option should never be used for heavily used programs and probably not for moderately used programs either.

USAGE=MAP

This parameter is used to specify that a map set or assembler program is to be loaded into map storage. Coding USAGE=MAP means that the program or map will be deleted from the Dynamic Storage Area (DSA) as soon as it is no longer in use. There may be some justification using it for low usage maps or assembler programs where virtual storage constraints are being experienced.

The System Initialization Table (SIT)

The SIT contains a vast assortment of parameters, some of which have a direct bearing on performance. Parameters can be overridden at CICS start-up time either via control cards submitted in the CICS job stream or by interaction with the system operator. Some parameters can be changed dynamically while CICS is running through the CEMT transaction.

AKPFREQ=0|number

This parameter is used to specify the activity keypoint frequency. CICS will take a snapshot of the system at certain times to enable it to perform an emergency restart should it be necessary. This activity keypoint is a record of in-flight tasks and the status of CICS tables at the time. AKPFREQ=0 means that no activity keypoints are to be taken and would only be used for a system which would never need to be emergency restarted. Otherwise, the value must be coded as a decimal value between 200 and 65,535. This value represents the number of blocks that are to be written out to the system log before an activity keypoint is taken.

Activity keypointing is a synchronous function and so prevents CICS from performing any other work while it is being done. There is also a strong likelihood of paging increasing while this is going on. This negative aspect of activity keypointing has to be balanced against the increased elapsed time of any emergency restart should the value be set too low. The *CICS Performance* manual suggests a value of between 200 and 2000, which is probably a bit too vague. Using CICS statistics, you should be able to calculate a value so that activity keypoints are being taken every 30 to 60 minutes.

AMXT=number

This parameter is used to specify the maximum number of active tasks that will be serviced by the CICS task dispatcher at any given time. The number can be any decimal value between 1 and 999, and if not specified will default to the value specified in the MXT parameter. By being able to limit the maximum number of tasks active in the system at any one time, the user can control the usage of both real and virtual storage. AXMT is discussed more fully in Chapter 3, How CICS Works, along with the related parameters MXT and CMXT.

BMS=....DDS|NODDS

If the DDS option of the BMS parameter is specified explicitly or by default, CICS will attempt to load a suffixed map set before trying to load an unsuffixed map set. Since most installations do not, in my experience, use suffixed map sets, CPU time can be saved by specifying BMS=NODDS.

CMXT=value1,value2,...,value10

This parameter is used to specify the maximum number of tasks of any particular class that can be in the system at any one time. The maximum value that can be specified is the lesser of 999 or the value of MXT; the minimum value that can be specified is 1. The values are coded positionally, the first value being the number of class 1 transactions that can be present and so on. It is the user's responsibility to assign the significance to these classes. For instance, class 1 transactions might be high priority transactions at one shop, while somewhere else class 1 might be reserved for trivial work. A more detailed discussion of this parameter plus the AMXT and MXT parameters can be found in Chapter 3, How CICS Works.

DBUFSZ=500|number

This parameter is used to assign a number of bytes to the dynamic buffer used for Dynamic Transaction Backout (DTB). If the buffer size specified is insufficient to hold the record that is being updated, temporary storage is used. Obviously, the implications of this will depend on whether auxiliary or main temporary storage has been specified in the Journal Control Program (JCP). If DTB=AUX is specified in the JCP and DBUFSZ is set low, a saving can be made in the amount of DSA used at the expense of increased I/O. In MVS/XA systems running CICS 1.7 or later, the DTB buffer is above the 16Mb line and should be set at a high value to prevent the buffer spilling onto temporary storage.

DLLPA=NO|YES (CICS/OS only)

This parameter is used to specify whether IMS modules are to be loaded in the MVS Link Pack Area (LPA) or not. Having the IMS modules in the LPA instead of the region's private area will reduce paging and real storage requirements. It may, however, impact other regions, since their maximum region size will be reduced by the amount of storage that these modules occupy.

DLMON=NO|YES (CICS/OS only)

This parameter is used to specify whether the IMS/DB monitor is to be turned on or not. Since this facility was designed to monitor IMS data bases in batch, it is unsuitable for use in CICS and should be left to default as DLMON=NO.

DLTHRED=1|number (CICS/OS only)

This parameter is used to specify the maximum number of IMS/DB users allowed at any one time. The maximum value allowed for DLTHRED is 255. If the value is set too low, transactions will have to wait; if the value is too high, both real and virtual storage will be wasted. Some degree of waiting may be unavoidable but it should be kept below 10% of all transactions. A number of sets of IMS/DB control blocks equal to the number specified in the DLTHRED parameter are set up at CICS initialization time. The size of these control blocks has increased with IMS/DB 1.3 from 3K to 9K.

DLXCPVR=NO|YES (CICS/OS only)

This parameter is used to page-fix ISAM and/or OSAM buffers. If you are one of the few remaining loyal ISAM or OSAM users and want to reduce paging at the expense of allocating more virtual storage, it would be wise to code DLXCPVR=YES. There is absolutely no point in VSAM-only sites coding anything but DLXCPVR=NO.

DMBPL=4|number (CICS/OS only)

This parameter is used to specify the number of 1K blocks of dynamic storage that are to be allocated for the Data Management Block (DMB) pool. Any number of blocks can be specified from 0 to 999. It is very important that you specify a high enough value because if CICS tries to access a data base and finds there is insufficient storage available, it will close the least recently used data base. This is clearly a situation that should be avoided at all costs. Assigning too high a value to DMBPL has no negative effect since any unused storage allocated to the DMB pool will be made available for other purposes. The DMB pool requirements for each data base are shown on its respective ACBGEN listing. I have always totaled these requirements for each data base in the system and rounded up to get the number of kilobytes needed. The only danger is that it is easy to forget this parameter when either your current data bases are changed or a new data base is introduced.

ENQPL=2|number (CICS/OS only)

This parameter is used to specify the number of 1K blocks of storage that are to be allocated for the IMS/DB enqueue pool. Any number of blocks can be specified from 0 to 999. The enqueue pool is taken from OSCOR storage and is used most heavily by DL/I transactions that use program isolation scheduling or scheduling by segment as opposed to by Program Specification Block (PSB), which is the majority. The enqueue pool is generally 2–3K at most installations. However, the consequences of running short are pretty unfriendly: the task will abend with a DL/I pseudo-abend code of U0775. This should obviously be avoided so code ENQPL=4, which should be more than adequate.

EXITS=NO|YES

This parameter is used to specify whether the CICS user exit interface is to be used or not. If you don't have any user exits, coding EXITS=NO or letting it default will save you some CPU time.

ICV=1000|number

This parameter is used to specify the amount of time in milliseconds for which CICS will relinquish control to the operating system in the event of it finding no work ready to run. ICV can be any value between 100 and 327,670. It can be used in low activity systems to prevent the CICS nucleus from being paged out. A rule of thumb would be between 5000 and 10,000 but would obviously vary considerably from installation to installation. The value for ICV must be equal or less than the ICVS value (see ICVS parameter).

ICVR=5000|number

This parameter is used to specify the amount of time in milliseconds that may elapse from the issuing of a CICS command after which CICS will deem a task to have "run away" and will issue an AICA abend. ICVR can be any value between 0 and 2700000. If ICVR=0 is specified, CICS will not attempt to detect run away or looping transactions. This time can be affected by higher priority partitions or regions and also paging; so a value should be selected carefully to avoid nonlooping transactions abending. The default value of 5000 is not such a bad place to start from.

ICVS=20000|number

This parameter is used to specify the amount of time in milliseconds for which CICS will wait before abending tasks defined as SPURGE=YES in the PCT after it has detected a system stress situation. ICVS can be any value between 100 and 327670 and cannot be any less than the ICV value. The lower this value is set, the quicker that CICS will be able to recover from a stress situation.

ICVSWT=40|number (CICS/DOS only)

This parameter is used to specify the amount of time in milliseconds for which CICS will relinquish control to the operating system while it waits for the completion of a short wait request, typically the completion of a disk I/O wait. ICVSWT can be any value between 0 and 1000. The length of the short wait should be just a fraction more than the length of time it completes an average disk I/O operation (i.e., 20–40 milliseconds), so a good setting would be ICVSWT=60. A value much lower than this would mean unnecessary CPU time being used checking for disk I/O completion, while too large a value will needlessly increase average response times.

ICVTSD=500|number

This parameter is used to specify the frequency in milliseconds between each attempt by CICS to process requests for terminal output. ICVTSD can be any value between 0 and 10,000. In BTAM systems it is a control on the frequency of full TCT scans invoked by terminal management. In VTAM systems, it regulates the speed with which terminal management processes VTAM requests. In VTAM-only net-

works with ICVTSD set low or to zero, output will be processed from
the activate queue chain, thus freeing resources earlier than if it had
to wait for a full scan of the Terminal Control Table (TCT). I would
recommend setting ICVTSD to 1000 in BTAM and mixed environments, and setting it to zero in VTAM-only shops.

IOCP=0|number (CICS/OS only)

This parameter is used to specify the percentage of events for which
CICS has issued an operating system multiple wait, which must
complete before it resumes processing. This percentage can be any
value between 0 and 50. Regions given a lower priority than CICS
will benefit if any value other than 0 is specified, but at the expense
of the CICS region. Let IOCP default to 0 unless it really is your
intention to give lower priority regions a performance boost.

LPA=NO|YES (CICS/OS only)

This parameter is used to specify whether CICS management
modules are to be loaded into the MVS Link Pack Area (LPA) or not.
Having the CICS management modules in the LPA instead of the
region's private area will reduce paging and real storage requirements. It may, however, impact other regions, since their maximum
region size will be reduced by the amount of storage that these
modules occupy.

MONITOR=ACC,PER,EXC

This parameter is used to specify which classes, if any, of monitoring
activity are to be collected. Use MONITOR=ACC for accounting
information, MONITOR=PER for performance information, and
MONITOR=EXC for exception information. This can be a very valuable source of CICS performance data, but it is obtainable at a high
price: gathering accounting information will increase CPU time by
up to 2%, exception information by up to 1%, and performance information by up to 18% for CICS/OS users and by up to 12% for
CICS/DOS users. The message is clear: only use this facility if the
information is really needed.

MXT=5|number

This parameter is used to specify the maximum number of tasks that can be present in the system at any one time. MXT can be set at any value between 2 and 999. By limiting the number of tasks, the requirements for virtual storage can also be reduced. MXT and the related parameters AMXT and CMXT are discussed more fully in Chapter 3, How CICS Works.

OPNDLIM=10|number (VTAM only)

This parameter is used to specify the number of concurrent VTAM logon and logoff operations that the system will accept. The lower the value defined for OPNDLIM, the lower the virtual and real storage requirements will be but at the expense of longer session initialization and termination. It is most effective when a large number of terminals have been defined with the CONNECT=AUTO option (see the CONNECT parameter), and there are times when the system is swamped by a lot of logon requests all at once. Individual requirements will have to be taken into consideration, although most sites will find the default value acceptable.

OSCOR=8192|number (CICS/OS only)

This parameter is used to specify the number of bytes of virtual storage that are to be released by CICS for use by the operating system. OSCOR can be any value between 0 and 16,777,215. Since the advent of CICS 1.7, OSCOR is used mainly to contain VSAM buffers and control blocks. Unfortunately OSCOR can be subject to a lot of fragmentation and is therefore a function of the amount of VSAM activity *and* the size and number of VSAM files rather than being directly proportional to the amount of VSAM buffer space.

PGSIZE=2048|4096

This parameter is used to specify whether 2K or 4K pages are to be used by CICS storage control. It is not as simple as specifying the page size used by the operating system (i.e., 2048 for VSE and 4096 for MVS). PGSIZE=2048 will improve the packing density of nonresident programs and maps in the DSA as these modules are loaded on page boundaries, although the probability of paging will slightly increase. Unless your nonresident programs are mostly very large and you don't have many of them, accept the default of PGSIZE=2048.

PISCHD=YES|NO

This parameter is used to specify whether program isolation scheduling is to be used with DL/I data bases or not. The alternative to program isolation scheduling or segment scheduling is intent scheduling. Program isolation scheduling enqueues on the segment and provides less chance of resource contention than intent scheduling, which enqueues on the Program Specification Block (PSB).

PLISHRE=NO|YES (CICS/OS and PL/I only)

This parameter specifies whether the PL/I shared library is to be used for common routines or not. Providing your common PL/I routines have been compiled with the SHARE option, you will save both on real and virtual storage by using the PL/I shared library.

PRGDLAY=hhmm

This parameter is used to specify how long BMS will wait to deliver a message to a terminal before it purges the message from temporary storage. The time is coded in hours and minutes: the hours can be any number between 0 and 99, while the minutes can be any number between 0 and 59. If this parameter is omitted or 0000 is coded, the message will remain ready for delivery until either it is purged or temporary storage is reinitialized. The message will tie up temporary storage for the length of time that it is left undelivered. This must be weighed against the suitability, or otherwise, of purging undelivered messages and will be dependent on each installation's business requirements.

PSBPL=4|number (CICS/OS only)

This parameter is used to specify the number of 1K blocks of dynamic storage that are to be allocated to the Program Specification Block (PSB) pool. The number of blocks specified can be any value between 1 and 999. The consequences of specifying too small a value are not too severe, although it will cause the least recently used PSB to be deleted from the pool. Specifying a value that is too large will not waste space in the DSA as the unused area will be made available for other purposes. The extra I/Os incurred by reloading PSBs have to be balanced against having a larger DSA and thus increasing the frequency of program compressions.

RAMAX=number (VTAM only)

This parameter is used to specify the size in bytes of the I/O area to be used for every VTAM RECEIVE ANY that CICS issues. RAMAX can be any value up to a maximum of 32,767. If the I/O area is insufficient to contain the message, additional buffers will be allocated. CICS will issue VTAM RECEIVE SPECIFIC instructions to read these extra buffers. If the value you assign to RAMAX is too high, you will waste both virtual and real storage; if the value you assign is too low, increased CPU time will be taken up acquiring additional buffers. Generally, a value equal to that specified in the RUSIZE parameter (see TCT RUSIZE parameter), namely 256, will satisfy the requirements of most installations and will certainly be adequate for 3270-only shops.

RAPOOL=2|number (VTAM only)

This parameter is used to specify the number of concurrent VTAM RECEIVE ANY requests that the system will accept. VTAM RECEIVE ANY requests are used to process unsolicited input from a terminal as opposed to VTAM RECEIVE SPECIFIC requests, which are used to process input that CICS is expecting. If RAPOOL is set too low, input messages will be queued by VTAM, which will cause longer response times. If RAPOOL is set too high, virtual storage will be wasted and CPU cycles will increase. If anything, it is better to be too high than too low. The *CICS Performance* manual suggests that you set RAPOOL to 1.5 times your transaction rate per second. This makes some sense. Most medium-to-large shops find the default value of 2 insufficient and choose a value somewhere between 5 and 20.

SCS=500|number

This parameter is used to specify the size in bytes of the storage cushion area, which CICS only uses when it has detected a short-on-storage condition. SCS can be any value between 20 and 524,288, although this value will be rounded up to be divisible by the page size specified in the PGSIZE parameter. CICS uses the storage cushion as a temporary measure to satisfy outstanding GETMAIN requests in an attempt to get tasks to complete and free up storage. If you are regularly hitting short-on-storage conditions, it is a symptom of another problem and it is there that you should concentrate your efforts. Setting SCS to the equivalent of seven pages, one for each subpool (14336 or 28672) is recommended.

SVD=0|number|YES|NO

This parameter is used to specify whether storage violation dumps are to be taken should storage violations occur, and how many of these dumps are to be taken. The number of storage violation dumps can be any value between 0 and 99. For production CICS systems, SVD should be set at 0 or at least a very low number, as storage violations should not occur in a live environment and should be investigated at once.

TD=3|number1,3|number2

This parameter specifies the number of buffers (number1) and the number of VSAM strings (number2) to be allocated to the intrapartition data set. Both values can be in the range 1–255 with 3 the default. If these values are set high, fewer tasks will need to wait for either buffers or strings but virtual storage consumption will increase. Start with the default values and adjust them if necessary, using standard CICS statistics, until waits are reduced to around 5% of all requests or eliminated altogether if you have sufficient virtual storage available.

TRT=0|number

This parameter is used to specify the number of entries that are to be contained in the trace table. TRT can be any value between 0 and 10,000. The CICS trace facility is a considerable overhead and will add about 20% to CPU times (each trace entry uses about 100 additional instructions) and should not generally be used on production systems.

TS=3|number1,3|number2

This parameter specifies the number of buffers (number1) and the number of VSAM strings (number2) to be allocated to the temporary storage data set. Both values can be in the range 1–255 with 3 the default. If number1 is set to 0, all temporary storage requests will be directed to main storage. If these values are set high, fewer tasks will need to wait for either buffers or strings but virtual storage consumption will increase. Start with the default values and adjust them if necessary, using standard CICS statistics, until waits are reduced to around 5% of all requests or eliminated altogether if you have sufficient virtual storage available.

TSMSGSET=4|number

This parameter is used to specify the number of entries that will be used for string pointers to records written to temporary storage message sets. TSMSGSET can be any value between 4 and 100. CICS statistics will list the number of TSMSGSET overflows, which should be around 20% of temporary storage writes.

VSP=NO|YES

This parameter is used to specify whether the MVS VSAM subtasking facility is to be used or not. The VSAM subtasking facility uses an alternative CPU in a multiprocessor environment to process VSAM, transient data, temporary storage, and journaling requests and so lighten the load on the main CPU. If the I/O of these categories is more than half your total I/O, you should definitely consider coding VSP=YES.

ZCP=NOHPO|HPO (CICS/OS only)

This parameter is used to specify whether the VTAM High Performance Option (HPO) is to be used or not. There is a slight integrity exposure with using this option, as not all normal auditing functions are performed. The performance gain is unquestionable.

The Sign-on Table (SNT)

The SNT contains entries for each operator-id that is to have access to the CICS system and is used to assign a password to that operator-id and to establish his or her security level.

OPPRTY=1|number

This parameter is used to assign a priority value to an operator. The number can be any decimal value between 0 and 255 and it is used in conjunction with priorities assigned at the transaction level (see the PCT TRNPRTY parameter) and at the terminal level (see the TCT TRMPRTY parameter) to arrive at a value which represents the task's dispatching priority up to a maximum value of 255. Giving different values at all three levels proves unworkable at most installations, and it is advisable that you only use one of the three. Which one you use will depend on your own particular circumstances.

The Terminal Control Table (TCT)

The TCT contains entries for all the terminals in a CICS system. There is a temptation to define every terminal on a network in the TCT, and I have even seen cases where TCT entries were generated for empty ports in the belief that they would be used at a later date and to prevent reassembling a new TCT when the day came. As each TCT entry uses about 500 bytes of virtual storage, a more accurate assessment of an installation's present and future terminal requirements would have been much more beneficial, although with CICS 1.7, VTAM terminals can be allocated dynamically and TCT entries built using RDO.

BUFFER=number (VTAM only)

As a TYPE=TERMINAL parameter, this is used to specify the maximum size in bytes of the data length that the device can receive. The maximum value that can be coded is limited by the physical characteristics of the device involved. For 3270-type devices, the recommended values are:

```
TRMTYPE=LUTYPE2     1536
TRMTYPE=LUTYPE3      256
TRMTYPE=SCSPRT       256
```

This parameter is only applicable to SNA devices. CICS will set BUFFER to 0 for VTAM non-SNA devices.

CHNASSY=NO|YES (VTAM only)

This parameter is used to specify whether or not complete chains of the individual elements, which make up terminal input, are to be assembled and passed to the application. There are, of course, performance implications concerned with the use of this parameter, although terminal characteristics will force CHNASSY=YES or CHNASSY=NO in many cases. CHNASSY should not be specified for non-SNA devices. CHNASSY=YES must be coded on 3270-SNA devices for BMS to function correctly.

CONNECT=AUTO (VTAM only)

This parameter is used to specify whether a VTAM session is to be initiated between the terminal and CICS when CICS is started. In a medium to large network, this can be a very time-consuming operation if not restricted by the OPNDLIM parameter.

GMMSG=NO|YES (VTAM only)

This parameter is used to specify whether or not the CICS "good morning" sign on message is to be displayed at the terminal. The obvious user friendliness of such an action must be balanced against the impact of having the system very heavily loaded at system initialization time.

NPDELAY=number (BTAM only)

This parameter is used to specify the number of milliseconds between polls of terminals defined on a BTAM OPENLIST when a negative response has been detected. NPDELAY can be any value between 0 and 20,000. OPENLIST polling is generally discouraged, although it is the only method of BTAM polling available to MVS users running under VM. Under these circumstances, use a value of around a 1000. If used, NPDELAY should not be set lower than the ICV parameter in the SIT (see ICV parameter in the SIT).

RETRY=7|number (BTAM and CICS/DOS only)

This parameter is used to specify the number of times that CICS will retry an operation should it encounter an I/O error. My experience with BTAM is that if an I/O error is not recovered after two or three retries, it will not be recovered at all. Code RETRY=3 and avoid some of the overhead of the additional CPU time used by retrying failing I/Os.

RUSIZE=256|number (VTAM only)

This parameter is used to specify the size in bytes of the Request Unit (RU) for the terminal and is used to satisfy VTAM RECEIVE requests. Most installations will find the default value of 256 adequate for their needs.

TCTUAL=number

This parameter is used to specify the size in bytes of the user area associated with this terminal. TCTUAL can be any value between 0 and 255. As its name implies, the TCTUA can be used in many various ways. Its length should be as small as possible with a small percentage reserved for future uses. The overallocation of TCTUAL will obviously have the greatest impact in larger networks, where the additional space, when multiplied by the number of terminals on the system, can result in considerable amounts of virtual storage that will never be used.

TIOAL=number,number

This parameter is used to specify the minimum size in bytes of the inbound message buffer that will be obtained by CICS for transactions associated with this terminal. For SNA terminals, the maximum size of the buffer can also be specified. The minimum size should be determined as the next value above the size of the average message, which is a multiple of 64, minus 16 for the Storage Accounting Area (SAA). Similarly, the maximum size should be determined as the next value above the maximum message size, which is a multiple of 64, minus 16.

TRMPRTY=0|number

This parameter is used to assign a priority value to a terminal. The number can be any decimal value between 0 and 255, and it is used in conjunction with priorities assigned at the transaction level (see the PCT TRNPRTY parameter) and at the operator level (see the SNT OPPRTY parameter) to arrive at a value which represents the task's dispatching priority up to a maximum value of 255. Giving different values at all three levels proves unworkable at most installations, and it is advisable that you use only one of the three. Which one you use will depend on your own particular circumstances.

5

The Effects of CICS Performance

This chapter looks at how much damage a badly performing CICS system can cause. It examines some of the reasons for poor performance and their cascading nature. The often overlooked area of the human interface is discussed, and the final section goes on to emphasize the importance of setting maintainable performance objectives and how to set up service level agreements with end users.

The Consequences of Bad Performance

When optimum use is not made of the hardware and software available, the company's profitability is going to suffer. Mainframe computers and their accompanying software are too valuable a resource to be allowed to fall short of their true capabilities.

The implications of both good and bad design are the same for CICS systems as they are for any other on-line applications. Substandard performance is felt mostly, and has the most adverse effect on an organization's profits, when the end-user is a customer, as in an on-line banking system; or when a member of staff is using CICS to order a service on behalf of a client, as in an airline or hotel reservation system, for example. Nobody likes to be kept waiting in today's high-speed world, especially if they are on the paying end of a telephone. If your system cannot give them timely response, they may well go off and find a system that will.

That is not to say that fellow company employees can be allowed to wait. It may not be quite so critical for them to be serviced in as timely a fashion as paying customers, but there have been several instances of badly designed on-line systems contributing to the lack of job satisfaction among the terminal operators using them and the consequent high turnover of staff.

When CICS is not running to specification, the help desk will be flooded with angry telephone calls from irate users and the credibility of the entire data processing operation will be questioned. The matter will raise its ugly head at departmental meetings with the possible outcome that a CPU upgrade can be postponed no longer.

Many organizations operate in this way. CICS is installed, sometimes at the request of a user department for the sole running of a particular application. Often this takes the shape of a package from an independent software vendor. At first, there is more than enough capacity on the CPU to cope with the early demand. Then further applications are added and CICS starts to creak a little. The next thing you know is that performance has deteriorated to such an extent that response times at the terminals are no longer acceptable to the users.

The machine is upgraded and we find CICS once again managing to provide the required service, but not for long. The load will gradually build up again until the entire cycle is repeated.

Many installations adopt this *react mode* method of operation instead of adopting a more predicative approach. On most CICS systems there is a great deal of scope for improving performance by tuning the system and, in so doing, to effectively postpone CPU upgrades by many months and, in some cases, by years. In addition, regular performance monitoring can mean that the requirement for an upgrade can be forecast more accurately, which means a more controlled and smoother transition.

Interfacing with Humans

An important factor in CICS performance that is all too often under-estimated or even totally overlooked is the actual human interaction with a particular CICS application. The effect that a non–user-friendly system can have on the workload can be enormous even if the programs themselves are not written inefficiently.

While this problem is not confined only to CICS, it is something that is felt most deeply in on-line work. Studies have shown how the work rate of a highly skilled terminal operator will drop at an alarming rate should he or she be made to work on badly designed terminal displays and be subjected to unhelpful messages. The terminal operator will develop a feeling of resentment towards the system which, in extreme cases, can even affect the individual's health and well-being. Most operators pride themselves on their speed and keyboard skills and view unfavorably any attempt to undermine this.

If you compare the two output displays shown in Figures 5-1 and 5-2, you will note how much more user friendly Figure 5-2 is than Figure 5-1. Figure 5-1 could well result in the terminal operator scurrying to the user manual to find the cause of this unhelpful error message if it is one with which he or she is unfamiliar.

Figure 5-2, on the other hand, is much more helpful — perhaps even a little overelaborate. It offers the novice the option of getting further information without leaving the terminal.

While Figure 5-2 is probably more representative of CICS applications in the majority of installations today, user friendliness does have its price. The logic of the program is considerably more complex to produce the second example — it could well involve one additional program and map. In addition, the amount of data that would be transmitted to the terminal is also much lengthier.

Certainly if the terminal operator can rectify incorrect input at the first attempt rather than requiring several attempts to put it right, then the more "wordy" approach outscores the "briefer message" method. Alternatively, a long description of the error couched in patronizing tones stands a very good chance of irritating the "old hand."

A great deal of thought must be given to ensuring that the type of message matches the operator's level of skill. In the real world, extremes of both sorts of screen design are to be found varying from the curt to the verbose, driven by the designer's perception of the end-user's abilities.

As well as not treating the terminal operator as an idiot, it is important to appreciate the effect that bad response time has on the

```
  CUSTOMER MASTER FILE ADDITIONS


CUSTOMER NUMBER:    87231

CUSTOMER NAME: MIKE RAWLINGS

CUSTOMER ADDRESS: 23 HIGH STREET

               SWINDON

               WILTS

               SN1 1AB



ERROR INVALID DATA
```

Figure 5-1   Example of a terminal error display.

individual. Detailed studies have revealed that excessive terminal wait times cause the operator not to perform at his or her best. Depending on the personality of the operator, he or she may experience any of a number of different emotions varying from panic, distrust, contempt, anger, etc. All will cause some degree of frustration and impact the effectiveness of a transaction. It is also more than likely that higher than normal error rates will be experienced, and this too will degrade overall performance by increasing the load on the CPU.

Many installations, in trying to defer an inevitable CPU upgrade, look at terminal response time and argue that a second or so on top of the existing figure is not going to make that much difference. They

```
           CUSTOMER MASTER FILE ADDITIONS


   CUSTOMER NUMBER:    87232

   CUSTOMER NAME: PAT KERSEY

   CUSTOMER ADDRESS: RAILWAY TAVERN

                     12 FARMSIDE ROAD

                     OXFORD

                     OX1 1CD

   YOU HAVE ENTERED A CUSTOMER NUMBER
   OUTSIDE THE RANGE 10000-59999 CORRECT
   THE CUSTOMER NUMBER AND PRESS ENTER TO
   CONTINUE, PRESS PF1 FOR FURTHER
   INFORMATION, OR PRESS PF12 TO RETURN TO
   THE MAIN MENU.
```

Figure 5-2   Example of a terminal error display.

are invariably proved wrong and probably lose much of their credibility and goodwill with their end-users as a result.

The Causes of Poor Performance

Slow response is undoubtedly the most obvious symptom of poor performance and is usually an indication of the overcommitment of one or more of a system's resources. Either insufficient storage (virtual or real) has been allocated, or there is contention on some I/O device or channel, or the processor is just not powerful enough to cope with the demands being made of it. Quite often, pressure on any one of these resources will have a "knock on" effect and manifest itself somewhere else.

CICS statistics will reveal many clues as to what has gone on during a particular CICS run. Things to be especially aware of are: the number of program compressions, the number of times the system reached the maximum number of tasks specified in the MXT parameter, the maximum number of active tasks, and the number of times a short on storage (SOS) condition arose.

It is also important to ascertain whether the response times are always slow, whether they are slow at peak times of the day, or whether inconsistent and erratic response times are being encountered. You must determine also whether all transactions are being affected, whether only certain categories of transaction are affected, or whether only transactions of a particular class are affected. Likewise you must investigate whether the problem is confined solely to local terminals, or to remote terminals, or both.

Other symptoms that can show themselves are transaction abends on normally stable applications, CICS itself abending, or the CICS system solidly deadlocked and just idly sitting there. It is a little ironic that the tolerance built into CICS, whereby a task will as a first step wait on resources rather than abending, can on occasions prove to be one of its failings.

Performance Objectives and Service Level Agreements

It is pointless to undertake any CICS performance tuning exercise without being able to compare the results with preset clearly defined performance objectives. In the absence of negotiated service level agreements between the computer center and its end-users, internal performance objectives should be set; then those responsible for CICS performance will have clear targets to aim for and maintain.

For a service level agreement to have any potency, it should accurately reflect the current and short-term future business needs of the enterprise. It should define a minimum level of operation to be maintained by the computer center and below which the company's profitability will suffer.

The agreement should be phrased in such a way that neither party is in any doubt as to what it represents. By this I mean that the document should be worded in plain language with computer jargon used only where necessary, and then fully explained within the context that is used.

A service level for CICS users can be incorporated into a more general agreement, although the definitions relating to CICS will probably need to be more precise.

The main components of the service level agreement that need to be defined are:

- The hardware
- The software
- Guaranteed response times
- Maximum number of transactions per hour that can be serviced
- The maximum size of data base files
- Hours of the day during which CICS will be available
- Periodic reports that will be available to monitor service

The Hardware

Where the computer center has more than one CPU, the lowest rated CPU on which the users work will be run should be defined as the basis for the service level agreement. The types of direct access storage devices (DASD), the terminal types, and controllers should also appear in the document. Define the back-up configuration carefully, and emphasize that performance on dial-up lines will not match that of nonswitched lines.

The Software

The release levels of all the relative IBM and non-IBM software should be clearly defined. The company's philosophy on software maintenance will have to be incorporated in this document as well as general guidelines for the implementation of new releases of software. It may be useful to isolate software with an erratic performance profile so that it does not interfere with better-behaved applications.

Guaranteed Response Times

The problem here lies in the difference between CICS internal response times and the actual response times experienced at the terminal. On remote terminals attached via busy lines, the two figures can differ enormously, sometimes to such an extent that it would make CICS internal response times practically worthless in trying to appease an irate end user.

There are hardware monitors on the market that will give an accurate indication of terminal response times. They use a dedicated mini-computer or PC to trap this information. The leading manufacturers of such equipment include Avant-Garde Computing, Inc., Data Communications Management Sciences, Dynatech Data Systems, Encom Corporation, and Questronics, Inc. IBM offers Response Time Monitor (RTM), which is implemented by adding extra micro-code to the $3x74$ cluster controller.

If the data processing department's budget will not run to such a monitor, you will have to determine and agree to some correlation between the response times perceived by the terminal operator and the internal response times reported by CICS.

Transactions should be grouped to reflect their different characteristics. If transactions are given priorities in the PCT, then a typical range of transactions might be: conversational transactions, printer transactions, high-priority transactions, medium-priority transactions, and low-priority transactions. Each group of transactions should have a guaranteed response time. If priorities are assigned in the SNT and/or the TCT in addition or instead of in the PCT, then all possible combinations of priorities should be defined and assigned a guaranteed response time. In practice, assigning multiple priorities often proves unworkable and is best avoided.

The usual agreement concerning response times is expressed as an installation providing a guaranteed response time for a certain percentage of transactions although a response time could be guaranteed 100% of the time subject to no other defined thresholds being exceeded.

Maximum Number of Transactions Per Hour That Can Be Serviced

Using the transaction groups as defined above, each group of transactions would have its own transaction rate. If the maximum transaction rate is exceeded, then obviously the negotiated response times cannot be guaranteed.

The Maximum Size of Data Base Files

The anticipated size of all the data base files allowing for growth must be known by the computer center if it is to function effectively. If files are allowed to grow unchecked, so too will the related resource consumption.

Hours of the Day During which CICS Will Be Available

The times at which CICS will be available to users should be laid down. It is important to take into account weekends and public holidays. The level of technical support that is available at any given hour should be incorporated. This level could be full support during normal office hours and call-out support or no support at other times and at weekends.

Periodic Reports that Will Be Available to Monitor Service

Ideally these should be kept to a minimum to be effective. Histograms and bar charts are probably the best types and should reflect all aspects of the service level agreement. Different reports will go to different individuals. Make sure people only receive information of direct relevance to their duties, otherwise they are likely to ignore the reports they are sent and dispatch them to the wastepaper bin.

Reviewing Service Level Agreements

Service level agreements should be reviewed periodically by all concerned parties. Ideally, some sort of penalties should be attached to the computer center, which should be exacted should they fall short of the agreement. This is fairly straightforward if there is some sort of chargeback mechanism but otherwise end-users may only be satisfied with the data processing manager's head. Certainly, someone must be accountable to the end users for any failures of the data processing department to meet any part of the service level agreement. Figure 5-3a and 5-3b illustrate how a service level agreement might look.

SERVICE LEVEL AGREEMENT

Between Computer Services and Accounts Payable Division for on-line
services via CICS.

23 June 1988

HARDWARE

On-line services will be supplied using the following equipment:

CPU: IBM 4381-2
DASD: 12 x IBM 3380-D
Communications controller: IBM 3725-2

linked to the following equipment installed in the Accounts Payable
Division offices:

12 x IBM 3179-1 display terminals
2 x IBM 3287 terminal printers
1 x IBM 3174-61C cluster controller

Communication will be over line FX70480 (9600 bits per second)
or, in the event of failure, over dial-up line (1200 bits per second).

SOFTWARE

IBM software
    MVS/SP Version 2.1.2
    CICS/OS/VS Version 1.7.0
Accounts Payable software
    Enquiries
        APS010 Version 2
        APS011 Version 2
        APS012 Version 2
        APS013 Version 3
    Additions
        APS020 Version 1
        APS021 Version 3
        APS022 Version 2
        APS023 Version 3
        APS024 Version 3
    Deletions
        APS030 Version 2
        APS031 Version 2
        APS032 Version 1
    Printing
        APS040 Version 5
        APS041 Version 3

Figure 5-3a   Example of a service level agreement (1 of 2).

GUARANTEED RESPONSE TIMES

Transaction name	Maximum response time	Maximum no. of transactions/hour
APS1	2 secs	500
APS2	2 secs	500
APS3	5 secs	200
APS4	3 secs	400
APS5	5 secs	100
APS6	2 secs	500
APS7	5 secs	150

Transaction name	Lines per minute
APS8	200
APS9	200

95% of all transactions will be processed within the specified response times or at the specified printer rate providing the volumes specified in this agreement are not exceeded.

DATA BASE FILES

	6/88	12/88
SUPPLIERS.FILE	500 cylinders	600 cylinders
ORDERS.FILE	100 cylinders	120 cylinders
DEPT.FILE	50 cylinders	50 cylinders

HOURS OF SERVICE

Mondays	08.00 - 18.00
Tuesdays - Thursdays	07.00 - 18.00
Fridays	07.00 - 17.00

REVIEW OF SERVICE LEVEL AGREEMENT

This service level agreement will be reviewed before 23 December 1988.

Figure 5-3b Example of a service level agreement (2 of 2).

6

Application Design

This chapter lays down some of the ground rules for the programming standards necessary to obtain good performance. The chapter progresses from general guidelines to more specific suggestions relating to COBOL, PL/I, and Application Generators.

Program Structure

Neither COBOL nor PL/I were designed primarily for on-line use. Both languages have their roots in batch processing, and as a result neither is ideally suited to CICS. The same can of course be said of Assembler and RPGII, probably more so in the case of RPGII. I make this point because it needs to be appreciated that *programming standards, if they have been based on a batch environment, are not always applicable to the on-line world in general, and to CICS in particular.* There are many potential traps for the unwary programmer to fall into should he or she try to apply a technique designed for batch operation to an on-line situation.

I know of one installation which decided to standardize on the COBOL compiler options FLOW and STATE. These options serve no beneficial purpose under CICS; indeed the application programmer's reference manual does in fact point out that they should not be used.

Their use is not, however, forbidden and they will cause a program that has been compiled with them to consume around 1200 bytes of additional storage. It is altogether too simple to take an existing procedure, used for batch programs, and adapt it to make it fit the needs of an on-line system without assessing the implications of all the compiler options. Many installations might benefit from a review of the compiler options that they use, particularly if they are basically the same for both batch and on-line programs.

Program Flow

I do not have the qualifications to enter into a debate on whether to use structured programming techniques or not. My background in computing is such that I remain purely an interested spectator when such matters are discussed. I would simply point out that, purely in performance terms, applications written using nonstructured techniques will generally be more efficient than structured programs. This is because the flow of a structured program will tend to deviate more often from a sequential flow and *increase the probability of paging*. This benefit must, however, be weighed against the obvious advantages and savings in application development and program maintenance that are to be had by employing structured techniques.

Should you be tempted, like Little Red Riding Hood, to stray from the direct path, try to make the subroutine more substantial than it would be if the program was written for batch execution. Attempt to place your subroutines in an order of probability of usage, with those most often used closest to the main line to increase the probability of it occupying the same virtual storage page. Try to avoid having subroutines that branch to other subroutines.

Exec Handle Condition

For a CICS program to be considered as truly structured, the EXEC HANDLE CONDITION statement should not be used to test for abnormal or error conditions. Its GOTO DEPENDING UPON logic breaks all the rules laid down by structured programming purists.

There is a strong case for writing your own error handling routines by coding EXEC CICS HANDLE ABEND(xxx) and bypassing the

need for the CICS calls that result from invoking an EXEC HAND-
LE CONDITION statement. Not only will you be able to write structured code, but you will be able to design your own standardized
abnormal condition processing incorporating more descriptive error
messages and problem diagnosis. You will also incur some reduction
in processing time by dispensing with the CICS calls.

The main disadvantage of creating your own routines is that, because they will need to be complex routines, they might well be subject to considerable changes in subsequent releases of CICS. It would
clearly be unwise to invest too heavily in writing routines that might
have to be thrown away or may be the cause of a lot of rewriting
should you upgrade your software.

RESP and RESP2

A welcome enhancement to CICS was introduced in Release 1.7 with
the addition of the RESP and RESP2 options. RESP and RESP2 can
be used with any EXEC CICS command and are used to address two
data areas designed to trap the CICS response to that EXEC CICS
command. The use of EXEC CICS HANDLE CONDITION and RESP
is illustrated in Figures 6-1 and 6-2. RESP2 is provided to enable
secondary response codes to be tested for. As can be seen from Figure 6-1 and 6-2, the same result can be obtained more easily using

```
EXEC CICS HANDLE CONDITION
     ENDFILE(CUSTMAST-EOF)
     END-EXEC
EXEC CICS READ
     DATASET('CUSTMAST')
     INTO(WS-CUSTMAST)
     RIDFLD(CUSTNO)
     END-EXEC
     .
     normal processing
     .
CUSTMAST-EOF.
     .
     end of file processing
     .
```

Figure 6-1   Use of EXEC CICS HANDLE CONDITION.

```
EXEC CICS READ
     DATASET('CUSTMAST')
     INTO(WS-CUSTMAST)
     RIDFLD(CUSTNO)
     RESP(READRESP)
     END-EXEC
 IF READRESP=DFHRESP(ENDFILE) THEN end of file processing
     ELSE normal processing
```

Figure 6-2   Use of RESP.

the RESP option without adding additional labels or using GOTO logic.

Summary

Strictly from a performance standpoint, then, CICS programs should follow as sequential a path as possible. Abnormal or error processing should be in either separate programs or in in-line subroutines. If you are determined to write structured code, be a little less rigid in your approach. You will have to make a few compromises in the interests of good performance. Be prepared to bend a little.

General Programming Guidelines

Program Size

I have heard a lot of arguments on the question of what is the optimum size for a CICS program. Installations that tried to standardize on a numeric value usually came up with a figure between 10K and 12K. However, the thinking on this subject has changed fairly dramatically over the past few years, especially among the MVS/XA shops.

These days it is no longer necessary to artificially break down programs into, say, 10K chunks, and 50K is probably a realistic limit in both terms of performance and maintainability. Certainly from a performance angle, one 50K program is better than five 10K programs unless you are one of these people who believes it is possible for nine women to have a baby in one month.

The functionality of an application should be the limiting factor on its size. Ideally, you should aim for a relationship of one program to one terminal interaction.

It is generally considered a better performance option to have bigger programs and increased storage demands than to incur the overhead involved with more frequent XCTLs and LINKs. Much depends on your environment, of course.

If your CICS system is dedicated to one application, it will be of much less importance than if you are running a large variety of different applications. With just one application running, you could have a program whose size would be considered absurdly high in a different environment. On the other hand, if your system contains a large number of different applications, it would be wise to break them down into several quite small programs.

Passing Control

When transferring control from one program to another, if you have a choice, it is far better to use XCTL than LINK. An XCTL only uses about a half of the CPU time of a LINK. In addition, the dynamic work area of any program that issues a LINK remains in storage, while a program that issues an XCTL frees up this storage. Another overhead incurred by LINKed programs is the requirement for a Register Save Area (RSA) to be generated. Therefore, if there is no need to return to the original program, always use LINK.

An alternative is to issue a CALL statement. This uses no CICS services and is therefore the most efficient way of transferring control between programs. The main drawbacks of such a method are that the CALLed program must be linked into the program that CALLs it, which prevents it being shared by other programs, except under special circumstances. This also means that the program must be relinked if the subroutine changes. If the CALLed program is a COBOL program, it must have been compiled with VS COBOL II to be able to issue CICS commands.

Data Handling

If you are writing command-level programs it is much better, again from a performance standpoint, to code constants or literals within your EXEC CICS commands rather than coding variables. Greater

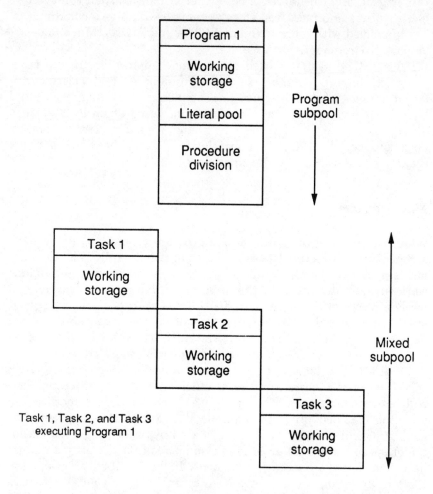

Figure 6-3   Working storage in the CICS environment.

efficiency is gained by having the data closer to where it is going to be used and thereby reducing the likelihood of paging. These imbedded constants will only be present once in the literal pool in storage, while copies of variables will occupy an area of storage for each task that is currently executing that particular program, as shown in Figure 6-3. If many users are simultaneously executing the same transaction, this overhead can be quite considerable. Again there is a trade-off of more efficient programs for more readable and more maintainable programs.

The likelihood of paging will also be greatly reduced if you wait until you are about to use an area of data before initializing it rather than, say, at the beginning of your program.

Processing the Date and Time

It is well worth giving some thought to your use of date and time constants in CICS programs. With releases of CICS prior to 1.7, the constants in the Exec Interface Block (EIB) EIBDATE and EIBTIME should be adequate for most sites' needs, using the EXEC CICS ASKTIME command, if necessary, which will cause EIBDATE and EIBTIME to be updated to reflect the current situation. From release 1.7, the ABSTIME option can be used with the EXEC CICS ASKTIME command to obtain the current date and time from the system and in conjunction with the EXEC CICS FORMATTIME command it can be used to obtain both time and date in whatever format the installation requires. COBOL's CURRENT-DATE uses the operating system services to extract a value and is best avoided.

Move Model I/O or Locate Mode I/O?

Move mode I/O and locate mode I/O are the two methods used by CICS command-level COBOL programmers to access data held on disk from their applications. The choice between the two methods is not as straightforward as it might appear at first sight, and it requires careful thought to ensure that the method appropriate to an installation's requirements and capabilities is chosen.

Move Mode I/O. Move mode I/O uses the working storage section to process CICS file requests. Figure 6-4 shows a code that might be used to invoke a read of a file by move mode I/O. The key thing to note is that the INTO option of the EXEC CICS READ command is used. Using this method, the control interval containing the record we want is read into the file's buffer area. The record is then moved into the working storage section of our program, where it can be processed by the task. It is important to appreciate that each task will have its own separate copy of working storage.

Locate Mode I/O. Locate mode I/O uses the actual address of the record in the VSAM buffer to process the file request. It does not physically move the record but instead keeps a pointer to it in the linkage section of the program. Figure 6-5 illustrates some code that might be employed to invoke a read of a file using locate mode I/O. Note that instead of using the INTO option on the EXEC CICS READ command the SET option is used.

Which to Choose? The two most important considerations that make locate mode I/O a more attractive proposition are:

```
WORKING-STORAGE SECTION.
77   CUST-KEY              PIC S9(9) COMP-3.
01   CUST-REC.
     05   CUST-NAME        PIC X(15).
     05   CUST-ADDR1       PIC X(30).
     etc
PROCEDURE DIVISION.
     .
     .
EXEC CICS READ DATASET('CUSTMAST')
     RIDFLD(CUST-KEY)
     INTO(CUST-REC)
END-EXEC.
     .
     .
```

Figure 6-4   Move mode I/O example.

```
WORKING-STORAGE SECTION.
77  CUST-KEY              PIC S9(9) COMP-3.
LINKAGE SECTION.
01  BLL-CELLS.
    05  FILLER            PIC S9(8) COMP.
    05  CUST-REC-ADDR     PIC S9(8) COMP.
01  CUST-REC.
    05  CUST-NAME         PIC X(15).
    05  CUST-ADDR1        PIC X(30).
    etc
PROCEDURE DIVISION.
     .
     .
     .
EXEC CICS READ DATASET('CUSTMAST')
     RIDFLD(CUST-KEY)
     SET(CUST-REC-ADDR)
END-EXEC.
     .
     .
```

Figure 6-5   Locate mode I/O example.

1. Less working storage is required using locate mode I/O since the record to be processed does not have to be moved into working storage to be processed. The amount of working storage involved can be quite sizable if the program is frequently executed by several concurrent users.
2. Locate mode I/O will use slightly fewer CPU cycles as there is less movement of data to be performed.

On the other hand, there are three main reasons why move mode I/O might be considered preferable to locate mode I/O. They are:

1. The majority of applications programmers find move mode I/O more straightforward and easier to code.
2. Move mode I/O is safer. With locate mode I/O, it is possible to corrupt CICS storage if the correct address is not loaded into the area's Basic Linkage Locator (BLL) cell.

3. When performing a simple read on a VSAM file, locate mode I/O ties up a VSAM string until the end of the task or until an UNLOCK command is issued, whereas move mode I/O releases the string as soon as the record has been moved into working storage.

Conversational or Pseudo-Conversational Programming?

It is generally accepted that pseudo-conversational programming is more efficient than conversational programming. In pseudo-conversational programming, resources are tied up for only a fraction of the time they are committed with conversational methods. With pseudo-conversational programming, CICS effectively uses the terminal operator's think time to process other tasks. This means that performance monitoring can be undertaken on a much more uniform and meaningful basis since this variable think time is eliminated from tuning statistics. Unfortunately, this is undermined to some extent by IBM's insistence on supplying conversational transactions such as CEMT, CESN, CECI, etc.

This is a great pity because a more serious problem that occurs with running both conversational and pseudo-conversational transactions together is that it becomes considerably more difficult to exploit the MXT and AMXT parameters to the full.

A case might be argued for using conversational techniques in a very high-rate data entry transaction where the input is being batched prior to some further processing by another application. By making the data entry transaction a conversational transaction, the overhead incurred by repeated security checking and other task initiation processing can be avoided.

Macro-Level or Command-Level Programming?

This should be a "no contest" given IBM's announced intention of phasing out macro-level programs or at least functionally stabilizing macro-level and increasing the functionality of command-level programs. Macro-level programs are much more difficult to code than command-level programs, with the applications programmer required to have some knowledge and appreciation of CICS internals and control blocks.

Be prepared, however, for a degradation in performance if you convert CICS applications from macro-level to command-level. It is very difficult to place an exact figure that would represent the result of such a conversion, but McCormack and Dodge Corporation, heeding IBM's message, rewrote their Application Development product Millenium 2 in command-level code instead of macro-level. The company found that the command-level code was some 20% less efficient than the equivalent macro-level code. Fortunately for MILLENIUM 2 users, McCormack and Dodge was able to recoup this shortfall by coding some modules in Assembler instead of COBOL.

COBOL Programming Guidelines

Command-level COBOL programs comprise more than half of all of the CICS application code currently executing at CICS installations. Today, its popularity is being challenged slowly but surely by Application Generators, but it still represents a considerable and ongoing investment for the majority of IBM mainframe installations. CICS COBOL Command-Level Application Programming is better covered by text books and courses than any other aspect of CICS. It is not the aim of this book to instruct you on this subject, and with this in mind the following section will only concern itself with the performance aspects of the most important areas of CICS COBOL programming.

COBOL Statements and Options to Avoid

At the beginning of this chapter I mentioned that COBOL was not designed primarily for the writing of on-line applications, and we have seen an example of the detrimental effect that bringing a batch facility into the on-line environment can have. There are many more traps waiting to catch out the unsuspecting applications programmer. It is quite allowable for an applications programmer to use any COBOL statement or any COBOL compiler option despite the obvious impact on performance some of them will have.

Many detrimental functions are self-explanatory given an appreciation of the fact that CICS provides its own file management and terminal management facilities and an understanding of how it does so. There is obviously no requirement for any of the entries connected with data files that would normally be found in either the Environment Division or the Data Division of a COBOL program.

CICS must also be allowed to access files through its own services and, therefore, the use of any of the file access statements such as READ, WRITE, OPEN, CLOSE, etc. are impracticable. Their use causes an operating system wait with the result that all CICS activity will stop and all transactions will be delayed.

Similarly, many of COBOL's special features were incorporated into the language with batch programs solely in mind, and whose use under CICS will have a detrimental effect on performance. Two obvious ones are SORT and REPORT WRITER, although you can add to this list ACCEPT, DISPLAY, EXHIBIT, SEGMENTATION, TRACE, and UNSTRING.

An installation made an exception to this last rule using DISPLAY UPON CONSOLE to put out a message to the operator's console in the event of a program detectable error occurring in a program defined in the PLT executed at CICS start-up time. Under these circumstances, and because Terminal Control would not be available at this time, I see no objection and consider it quite a sensible thing to do.

We have already seen what the effect of using the COBOL compiler options STATE and FLOW can be. To these two options you can add COUNT, ENDJOB, DYNAM, SYMDMP, SYST, and TEST.

Once a program has been transferred to a production CICS system, I would recommend using the OPTIMIZE compiler option to generate optimized code. In most cases this will reduce the size of the program by between 5 and 10%. Even more beneficial would be to use a third party product, such as CA-OPTIMIZER from Computer Associates International, Inc., where the benefits would be even greater.

COBOL Functions to Avoid

Two COBOL functions that will have an adverse effect on performance are the EXAMINE and variable MOVE operations. Both of these will incur the additional processing overhead of being expanded into subroutine calls if they are invoked.

An effective way of making sure that IBM standards are stuck to and to see to it that installation standards are followed is to write your own front-end processor to scan the source code before passing its output on to the CICS COBOL preprocessing program. It does, of course, impose the overhead of an additional batch program for each compilation, but it has enormous possibilities. It can reduce overall batch CPU time if it cancels the job should the first step not meet with a satisfactory outcome.

The COBOL REDEFINES Clause

Where possible, consider using the COBOL REDEFINES clause to reuse areas in Working Storage. Again, this will have to be weighed against making the program less readable and maintainable.

The COBOL RES Option

I stated earlier that there were special circumstances under which a CALLed program does not have to be linked into the program that CALLs it, and this is so when a COBOL program is compiled with the RES option. The RES option ensures that the CALLed program is not loaded until it is first used and can then be shared by any other COBOL program.

PL/I Programming Guidelines

Many of the techniques described in the section on COBOL Programming Guidelines apply equally to programs written in PL/I. The logic and reasoning applied to the use or nonuse of a particular statement, command, option, etc. is just as valid when applied in the PL/I environment. Only the names have been changed.

PL/I Functions to Avoid

As CICS does its own multi-tasking and as CICS itself controls it neither the PL/I multi-tasking built-in functions COMPLETION, STATUS, and PRIORITY nor the PL/I multi-tasking options PRIORITY, TASK, and EVENT should be used.

PL/I Statements to Avoid

CICS also handles its own file control, terminal control, and program control. For this reason there is no need for a CICS programmer to use any of the following PL/I statements: READ, WRITE, GET, PUT, OPEN, CLOSE, DISPLAY, DELAY, REWRITE, LOCATE, DELETE, UNLOCK, STOP, HALT, and EXIT. Similarly, if you are using the PL/I Optimizing Compiler, do not code FETCH or RELEASE.

Also at variance with the structure and architecture of CICS are the PL/I error handling routines and the internal PL/I sort. Their use should be confined to batch programs only.

The PL/I Shared Library

The PL/I equivalent to the COBOL RES option, which allows subroutines to be CALLed by a program into which they have not been linked, is the PL/I Shared Library. All manuals, text books, articles, and papers that I have read on the subject recommend its use. I am not going to disagree with them.

PL/I Program Storage

CICS will keep only one copy of a PL/I program's Static Storage, while its other storage areas will be present once for every current task that is executing that particular program. Therefore, it makes good sense to define all literals and constants in PL/I Static Storage.

Data areas should be reused as far as possible without seriously damaging the program's legibility and its overall clarity. In PL/I, this can be done by using Based Storage.

In data structures, the individual elements should be defined in the approximate order of their use to obtain best performance. In PL/I, since arrays are stored by row, it makes good sense to define arrays so that they can be processed by row rather than by column.

The Use of Application Generators

Recent research shows that nearly 60% of CICS installations make some sort of use of Application Generators to produce their CICS

File Placement

One of the prerequisites for the job of data administrator should be the absence of a tidy mind. The placement of CICS files, whether they be VSAM files or data base files, will often prove to have a detrimental effect on performance if these files are nicely grouped. Having all the personnel files on one volume and the accounts files on another may simplify security and make backing up easier, but it will, almost certainly, bring with it data set contention problems.

Another dilemma that frequently occurs is whether to optimize the usage of a DASD volume or not. If a CPU is devoted mainly to processing one CICS system, then the fullest use of DASD capacity cannot be had without impacting performance. It is a measure of the steadily improving price/performance ratio that, today, fewer and fewer sites are filling DASD volumes to their full capacity.

The data administrator must also be fully aware of the interference that can be caused to a CICS system by files outside the direct control of CICS. Prime candidates for files that should not be placed on the same volume with any but the most lightly used CICS files are the page data sets, program libraries, compiler and sort work areas, and the spool files of either JES or VSE/POWER. Consideration must also be given to the CICS journal data sets, the auxiliary temporary storage data set, the transient data set, the auxiliary trace data set (if used), and, to a lesser extent, the dump data sets.

It is very common to see the data portion and the index portion of a VSAM KSDS data set residing on the same volume. Moreover, I have seen the two portions occupying space at opposite ends of a 3380 volume. As it happened, and purely by accident, the data set was not highly used by any CICS applications. If it had been, the consequences could have been horrendous.

Consider what would have happened during a normal access of a record, for instance. Each time the index was read, the 3380 would then have to move across more or less the entire length of the pack to position itself for the data and then the whole way back again if it needed to read the index again. If it is possible, try to define the data portions and index portions of VSAM KSDS data sets on drives that use different channels; this will give even better performance.

A simple method of determining good file placement is to capture the total file EXCPs of your CICS system over, say, a week. Make sure you take into account the CICS files that I have mentioned above. Add all these EXCPs together and divide by the number of different DASD volumes that you have available. Providing no one file has excessively more EXCPs than the rest, you can rearrange your data sets, trying to keep data and index portions of the same data set apart, so that they all reside on volumes with approximately the same total EXCP count. Once you have gotten to this stage, fine tuning becomes much easier.

Programming Considerations

It is important that a CICS applications programmer has a full knowledge of the various CICS file control commands available to him or her and appreciates their possible adverse impact on the overall running of the CICS system. He or she must take into consideration other CICS applications — something there would be no need to do in the batch environment. Once he or she has finished processing a particular file, it must be released immediately. Otherwise, other transactions that use the same file will be made to wait needlessly. The CICS applications programmer must be made to understand that his or her work will not run in isolation but is merely a cog in a wheel, a wheel which will benefit from being oiled by a consideration for others.

Enqueues

CICS performs enqueues on recoverable resources, such as VSAM data sets, to ensure that their integrity is maintained. In simple terms this means that CICS will not permit two tasks to update a resource at the same time. Enqueues last until the task terminates or until the task issues a SYNCPOINT to signal to CICS that the update is "committed," i.e., there is no going back.

The longer this enqueue lasts, the more chance there is of a second task requiring the resource that is enqueued upon. Good programming techniques should therefore insist that the length of time for which a resource is enqueued is kept to the absolute minimum.

Event 1   Task 1 issues a get for update on data set CUSTMAST, customer number 25000. CICS gives Task 1 exclusive control of this record.

Event 2   Task 2 issues a get for update on data set PRODMAST, product number 01010. CICS gives Task 2 exclusive control of this record.

Event 3   Task 1 issues a get for update on data set PRODMAST, product number 01010. Task 1 is suspended by CICS as Task 2 already has exclusive control of this record.

Event 4   Task 2 issues a get for update on data set CUSTMAST, customer number 25000. Task 2 is suspended by CICS as Task 1 already has exclusive control of this record. Both tasks are waiting for the other to complete and cannot continue.

Figure 7-1   A "deadly embrace" situation.

Deadlocks. Contention can also lead, in extreme cases, to resource deadlocks. This situation occurs when a task wants to update a protected resource held by another task, which in turn wants to update a protected resource held by the first task, as illustrated by Figure 7-1. To avoid this situation, an in-house convention needs to be established to make sure that protected resources are always updated in the same order.

Browsing Data Sets

Of all the facilities at the disposal of a CICS applications programmer, the one that makes the CICS performance analyst grow white with fear is the browse operation. Browsing provides the programmer with the opportunity of sequentially searching a data set and the potential for much more in terms of degrading overall response times.

If the data set is of any considerable size, this may prove to be a very expensive facility in terms of resource consumption. A VSAM string is required for each browse and this string could be tied up for a long time. During a browse operation, one I/O can satisfy several consecutive READNEXTs. These will be processed without passing control back to CICS and so will seriously impact other concurrent applications.

One method to prevent applications with long browses in them from hogging the CICS system is for the browsing program to issue an EXEC CICS SUSPEND before each READNEXT operation. This has the effect of allowing CICS to process other transactions more often during the browse and so speed up the overall throughput of the CICS system at the expense of the browse transaction.

One thing that a programmer must never do in a browse is to update a record during the browse. Both operations will require a VSAM string to function and this could easily bring about a dead-locked CICS system, especially if any other tasks have the idea of doing the same thing. If you want to update one of the records, always end the browse first.

READ FOR UPDATE

A piece of sloppy programming practice that I have come across is the use of READ FOR UPDATE on records which there was never any intention to change. READ FOR UPDATE not only uses more resources than a simple READ, but it enqueues upon that record. If the Dynamic Transaction Backout (DTB) option has been specified in the PCT for the particular transaction, an extended enqueue will be maintained until either a syncpoint is issued or the task finishes. This is because CICS will not permit another task to update that record until the task originally updating it has either successfully completed or has had its update backed out should it have terminated abnormally. This guarantees the integrity of the data set.

VSAM Considerations

When looking at VSAM performance under CICS and looking for ways to improve it, there are a number of items that we must investigate. They fall into two broad categories: VSAM definitions and FCT parameters. To arrive at appropriate values for these definitions and parameters, we must first have detailed knowledge of the files involved. In particular we need to know the likely size of the

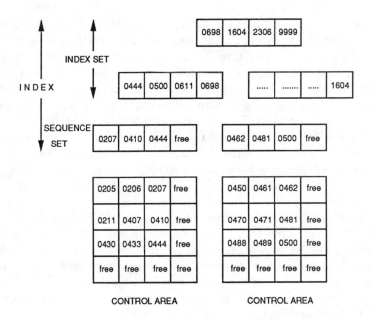

Figure 7-2   Structure of a VSAM index.

file, the type of processing that will be performed on the file (i.e., will the file be processed sequentially, will it be processed randomly, or both), and the frequency with which the file will be accessed.

Once we have the answers to these questions, then we can see if our current definitions and values are appropriate.

VSAM File Definitions

Control Interval Size (CISIZE). The CISIZE for both the data portion and the index of a VSAM KSDS data set is used by CICS to determine the relevant buffer sizes. CISIZE is VSAM's unit of transfer between the DASD and CPU. Standardizing on an appropriate value is good practice and especially recommended if the data set is participating in using Local Shared Resources (LSR) buffers. Figure 7-2 shows the index structure of a VSAM KSDS file.

A value of 2048, 4096, or 8192 for the data component should satisfy the requirements of most installations. Exactly which value to choose depends on what type of processing you expect to do on the data set. Generally a small CISIZE should be used for random processing to reduce the size of the I/O buffers, while better performance will be obtained for data sets that are frequently processed sequentially if the CISIZE is as large as possible.

If you are unsure about how the file will be used, it will generally be found to be slightly better to opt for a high CISIZE. The processing overhead associated with incorrectly defining a sequentially processed data set with a small CISIZE is greater than for incorrectly defining a randomly processed data set with a large CISIZE, although, of course, VSAM buffer requirements will be higher.

The CISIZE for the index component of a KSDS data set can have a considerable influence on CICS performance since each low-level index record contains a pointer to the data component. If the index CISIZE is set too small, it may not be able to contain sufficient pointers and as a result the data component's control areas will be underutilized and disk space will be wasted.

VSAM will calculate an appropriate index CISIZE if one is not specifically defined. While blindly accepting VSAM defaults is not to be generally recommended, in my experience this is one case where you can accept what you are given. The CISIZE will be calculated based on the data CISIZE, the data CASIZE, the key length, and the record length. In most cases this should prove adequate.

Control Area size (CASIZE). The CASIZE is not specified directly but is derived by VSAM from the information it obtains concerning the size of the data set's secondary allocation or primary allocation if no secondary allocation is given and the type of DASD that is being used. CASIZE can vary between one track and one cylinder in size, with one cylinder generally giving the best performance.

The main disadvantage of having a large CASIZE is that, should a Control Area split occur, there is much more data that needs to be shifted. This has to be balanced against the fact that the chances of a Control Area split occurring are reduced if CASIZE is high.

A large CASIZE will also mean fewer sequence set records and fewer levels of index. Having fewer levels of index is a considerable performance gain.

FREESPACE. The FREESPACE parameter is used to specify how much of a file is to be originally left empty for the subsequent addition of new records. It is defined as a percentage of the total size of the file. The value used in the FREESPACE definition is very much dependent on the processing characteristics of the file. The value will need to be high for files which experience a lot of insertions and can be set to zero for read only files. It should be carefully monitored to minimize Control Interval splits and to eliminate Control Area splits entirely.

If you have files where additions are not likely to be evenly distributed, it is possible to have varying amounts of FREESPACE throughout the file. This is achieved by taking a sequential copy of the file and then breaking down the reload of the file into sections. Use REPRO with the KEYRANGES option to reload the file and Access Method Services to ALTER the FREESPACE value before each load.

IMBED. If the IMBED parameter is used to define a KSDS file, the sequence set is written onto the first track of its respective Control Area. It will generally improve the performance of both sequential and random access to the file, at the expense of using the additional disk space to hold the copy of the sequence set.

REPLICATE. If the REPLICATE parameter is used to define a KSDS file, each record of the index set part of the index will be replicated as many times as it will fit onto a single track. This will improve performance by greatly reducing the rotational delay time on the disk containing the index at the expense of using additional disk space to achieve it. If the index set can be kept in core, this parameter is of no value and should not be used unless the data set is using the LSR pool. In these circumstances, the interference from other data sets using the same LSR pool will cause the index buffers to be flushed out more frequently. Here REPLICATE will be of considerable benefit. Figure 7-3 shows the effects of using IMBED and REPLICATE.

FCT Parameters

STRNO, BUFND, and BUFNI. These three parameters are the main controlling influence on file I/O buffers in CICS. They need to be

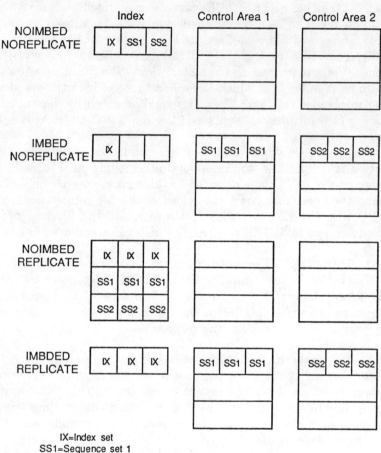

IX=Index set
SS1=Sequence set 1
SS2= Sequence set 2

Figure 7-3   The IMBED and REPLICATE options.

looked at together when determining appropriate values for them. In addition, details of the data set's size, usage, and processing characteristics need to be borne in mind.

The STRNO parameter is used to specify the number of strings that CICS is to support for this data set. A string is required for each concurrent access to the data set. If there are insufficient strings defined for a data set, subsequent tasks will be forced to wait until a string becomes available.

While it is a noble aim to reduce these "wait on strings," do not be preoccupied with their total elimination. A small number, for instance 5% of your I/Os for a particular file, should prove to be acceptable. It is better for a transaction to wait at this stage of its life than to let it proceed and run short of buffers.

The BUFND parameter is used to specify the number of data buffers that CICS is to allocate to this data set. CICS requires this to be set to at least STRNO+1 to cater for the processing of any possible Control Interval or Control Area splits that might arise.

If any additional data buffers are allocated, CICS will use them in any sequential processing that might occur against the data set and so allow I/O with the processing of the transaction. Unfortunately, this obvious performance gain has a slight sting in its tail inasmuch as CICS will allocate these additional data buffers to the first task to initiate sequential processing on the data set. Any other task wishing to perform sequential processing on the data set will be restricted to just one data buffer. This is, of course, far from equitable and you would be well advised not to allocate any additional data buffers to a data set unless sequential access to that data set is limited to one task at any one time.

The BUFNI parameter is used to specify the number of index buffers that CICS is to allocate to this data set. The minimum that can be specified is equal to the value specified in the STRNO parameter. This will prove inadequate in all but the smallest of data sets.

When CICS gets a request to process a data set, it employs what is called a "look-aside" technique. This means that before it goes off to the disk to retrieve the record, it first has a look in its buffers to see if it already has it. If it can satisfy the request from data that it is holding in its buffers, then no physical I/O occurs. Since we are typically dealing with fewer records when we deal with indexes, the chances of the "look aside" being successful are increased. Therefore, you should aim to hold as many index records in these index buffers as is practicable. You should be able to keep the high level index set record at least in storage, and with small data sets with few levels of index it might well be possible to keep all index records in storage.

The high level index set is just one record and to keep it in storage BUFNI should be set to STRNO + number of index levels.

Local Shared Resources

The VSAM Local Shared Resources (LSR) facility provides users with the capability of sharing the strings and buffers of VSAM data sets. If implemented wisely, it can greatly reduce the virtual storage requirements of a partition or address space as well as saving real storage.

IBM is so keen to get users to use the facility that from CICS 1.7 VSAM data sets use LSR by default rather than having to be explicitly defined to use it. In addition, the CICS System Definition data set, DFHCSD, is able to use LSR from CICS 1.7. These two changes follow on from CICS 1.6.1, which removed the restrictions on alternate index paths and base clusters with an upgrade set.

This shift of emphasis now means that the systems programmer should look at his CICS files and determine which are not suitable candidates for participating in LSR rather than looking for files which could benefit from using LSR.

There can be no denying the huge benefits to be gained in using LSR for all but the most heavily used files. This is increased if standardized CISIZEs are used as each different CISIZE uses a different subpool of LSR. It is good practice to use different CISIZEs for the data and index portions of a file so that they use different subpools.

It should be noted that LSR buffers will be overwritten by fresh buffers based on the least recently used algorithm. Any competition for buffers between the data and index components of the same data set will dramatically increase the chances of buffers being flushed out that could satisfy an imminent read request. Therefore, it is highly recommended that different CISIZEs for the data and index components be defined so that different subpools are used.

DL/I Considerations

The techniques for optimizing the performance of DL/I data bases under CICS closely follows the methods used with VSAM LSR files. The sharing of buffers under DL/I restricts most tuning activity to a global level, which can allow individual files to distort the usage of buffers under CICS. Allocating sufficient buffers for file I/O without incurring the overhead of excessive paging still stands as one of the tuner's primary aims.

As well as optimizing storage, the design of the data base and its application is an area that can have a negative influence on performance if badly done. The VSAM definition of the file(s) holding the data base also needs to be considered.

SIT Parameters

Under CICS/OS the CICS-DL/I interface derives the information it needs to set up its storage areas mainly from the SIT, namely the DLTHRED, DMBPL, ENQPL, and PSBPL parameters. The PISCHD parameter is also defined in the SIT. This parameter describes what type of data base scheduling is required.

DLTHRED. The DLTHRED parameter is used to specify the number of concurrent accesses or threads that will be supported through DL/I. If the figure is set too high, both real and virtual storage will be wasted. If it is set too low there is more chance of transactions being made to wait until threads become available leading to increased response times. Each thread uses about 9K bytes of storage, so good judgment is required to arrive at the most suitable figure for this parameter.

DLTHRED should be set high enough to ensure an even flow of DL/I tasks. Having no tasks ever waiting for threads would seem to imply that DLTHRED is set too high. Try to aim for a situation where around 5% of tasks are waiting for threads unless you don't have any storage problems.

DMBPL. The DMBPL parameter is used to specify how many 1K blocks are to be reserved from the DSA shared subpool for the Data

Management Block (DMB) pool. It is used to set a high water mark for allocation, and any overallocation in the definition can be used for other purposes. If too little storage is defined, the least recently used data base is closed in order to accommodate the data base CICS wants to access. There is no point at all in being tight so make sure that DMBPL is set high enough to prevent this happening. The ACBGEN output will give details of the DMB pool requirements, so it is a fairly straightforward matter to get this parameter right.

ENQPL. The ENQPL parameter is used to specify the number of 1K blocks that will make up the enqueue pool. This storage is taken directly from OSCOR. Enqueue control blocks are used more heavily in program isolation scheduling than in intent scheduling but a value of 4 should be more than adequate for most installations.

PSBPL. The PSBPL parameter is used to specify the number of 1K blocks to be reserved for the Program Specification Block (PSB) pool. Again this storage is taken from the DSA shared subpool. The minimum size of this pool should be the size of the largest PSB likely to be used times the DLTHRED value.

PISCHD. This should be specified as PISCHD=YES to invoke program isolation scheduling. Program isolation scheduling is preferable to the alternative of intent scheduling, since it enqueues on the data base segment and its dependent segments rather than on the PSB.

DL/I Application Programming Considerations

CICS-DL/I programmers are shielded from a great deal of the inner workings of both CICS and DL/I and can perform a great deal of their work with little or no knowledge of the internal structures of CICS or DL/I, although doing so will obviously lessen the efficiency of any code produced. A basic philosophy and a few simple do's and don'ts must be communicated to them to enable their programs to take fullest advantage of facilities available and to prevent any unnecessary overloading of the system's components.

The EXEC DL/I Interface. The EXEC DL/I interface, which was introduced in release 1.6 of CICS and which has been enhanced in subsequent releases, should always be used in preference to DL/I calls. Not only does it make programming considerably easier, but it also allows MVS/XA users to have DL/I programs loaded above the 16Mb line.

DL/I Paths. When coding DL/I applications it is also advisable to issue path calls wherever it is possible to do so. The alternative of invoking DL/I for each segment in the data base hierarchy will incur a far greater processing overhead.

PSB Scheduling. Any temptation to schedule the PSB at the start of a transaction and terminate it at the end should be avoided. While similar practices in batch are usual and acceptable, in CICS they can prove costly. The scheduling of the PSB should be delayed until the last possible moment and released as soon as it is possible. By doing this, the likelihood of more than one task enqueuing on the same data base record will be reduced considerably.

Data Base Design

In DL/I, the modification of one data base segment can cause many other, seemingly unconnected, segments to become involved in the process, as it is also necessary to update the pointers which hang the whole data base structure together. This can often compound the number of disk I/Os, and we often get the situation where a simple update to a data base segment has necessitated a string of further disk I/Os. Good design is about reducing these additional I/Os by the careful consideration of the nature of the data base.

HDAM Data Bases. If VSAM is used as the underlying file access method, an HDAM data base consists of a single ESDS data set containing all the data.

HDAM data bases use a randomizing algorithm based on the key of the data base record to calculate where the record should be physically located. If any record randomizes to a control interval that is already full, then it will store a pointer in that control interval and the record will be stored in the overflow area. This has serious consequences on performance and should be avoided. In addition, specifying free space for HDAM data bases is self-defeating as it will increase the probability of an inserted record randomizing to a full control interval.

HIDAM Data Bases.   If VSAM is used, an HIDAM data base consists of a KSDS data set to hold the root keys and pointers to the data and an ESDS data set containing the data. For this reason it is necessary to allocate the KSDS index, the KSDS data, and the ESDS portions as widely as possible.

If a lot of additions are to be made to the data base, an appropriate amount of free space defined in the DBDGEN macro and in the KSDS IDCAMS definition will be beneficial. If there are a lot of deletions on the data base, be sure to schedule frequent data base reorganizations.

Long Twin Chains.   Having long twin chains can considerably degrade performance as DL/I may be forced to scan several segments over a number of different control intervals in order to maintain the chain or to retrieve a segment. The easiest solution to this problem may well lie in the redesign of the data base. If the segments are small, it might be beneficial to combine a number of segments into one segment. Alternatively, a segment could be introduced at an intermediate level in the hierarchy. Unfortunately, in either case this will introduce additional complexity into any programs accessing the segments.

Another disturbing fact of life related to twin chains is that while their average record length may be a reasonable size, their maximum length can be excessive. Of course, it is often the most active records that have the longest twin chains.

8

Data Communications in CICS

This chapter takes a look at the flow of a transaction through the network with particular regard to where delays might occur and on what scale. Site options concerning the TCT, the automatic installation of terminals, BTAM settings, and VTAM and NCP parameter are also examined. The chapter goes on to look at network management issues relating to CICS and to discuss data stream compression giving details of the third-party offerings in this area. The chapter concludes with some advice on using BMS to obtain optimum performance from it.

Traveling the Network

If you put almost any CICS transaction under the microscope and examine it in detail, you will see that the largest part of its life is spent somewhere in the communications network. This is of course dependent on your having a tool installed which gives you the *actual* response time. By this I mean a tool capable of recording the amount of time taken between a user keying in data and hitting enter and receiving a response back at the terminal.

Sadly, many installations do not have such tools. This is not altogether surprising as this is an area of performance monitoring that has been badly neglected over the years. The fact that a communications network runs at all is considered sufficient at many sites, and its efficiency or otherwise is left unchecked.

The most popular method of obtaining actual terminal response times is by using IBM's Response Time Monitor, which is an additional function added to the micro code of the remote control unit to which the terminal is attached. Differences of up to fifteen seconds between internal response times as shown by CICS software performance monitors and response times recorded by IBM's Response Time Monitor have been reported.

Waiting on terminal I/O is a fact of life common to all on-line applications and is not peculiar to CICS. After all, we talk of instructions on the CPU in terms of millionths of seconds, file I/O is described in thousandths of seconds, while terminal I/O is measured in characters per second.

CICS interfaces well with all of the terminal access methods that it supports, namely, VTAM, BTAM, and TCAM and their derivatives, and it is probably true to say that most performance problems in this area can be laid at the door of the terminal subsystem and not be attributable to CICS itself.

Let's examine a typical transaction and see where the hold-ups are likely to occur. Let's assume we have a simple file enquiry in which the user enters a four character transaction-id followed by an eight-figure customer number and, as a result, is supplied at his terminal with a display showing all of the customer's details currently held on the customer master file.

As we are at a remote location, the initial message is transmitted from the terminal to a cluster controller (typically a 3x74) and then to our modem. From the modem, the message is sent over a line to a modem at the host location. It passes from this modem to a front-end processor or communications controller (typically a 37xx) and then on to the host mainframe, where the transaction is processed and the output screen built ready to be sent over the same route in the opposite direction back to the initiating terminal.

The first delay we experience is caused by waiting to be polled. VTAM and TCAM have their own methods of controlling polling and are outside CICS. For them polling is implemented by the NCP. This means that input for CICS transactions competes for network resources with other traffic, e.g., a CICS system of lesser importance, a TSO user, ADR/ROSCOE, or even IMS/DC. Any priority that CICS enjoys at the address space or partition level will have no effect on how VTAM or TCAM services transmission requests.

With BTAM, the method of polling is defined in the TCT entries for the line and terminal. Wrap-around polling is the recommended specification. This means that CICS will continuously scan the TCT looking for work.

The alternative is open list polling, which means that CICS will work its way down the TCT looking for input. If it does not find any, it will wait for the length of time specified in the NPDELAY parameter of the respective TCT LINE entry to elapse before starting another scan of the TCT.

The maximum permissible value of 20,000 for the NPDELAY parameter would add twenty seconds to our response time, and we haven't gotten as far as the control unit yet!

As our input message continues its journey, the next significant portion of time that we have to account for is the actual line time. Although faster lines are available, the most common transmission speeds are 4800 bits per second (bps) and 9600 bps for dedicated lines, and 1200 bps for dial-up lines.

Fortunately, our input is very short (it will be a different story on the way back) — even so, it would still take about one tenth of a second to get it over the line if we are using dial-up facilities.

Next we go to the communications controller, where we shall have to compete with other network traffic on an equal basis. This can easily become a major bottleneck, although it is an area outside of the immediate responsibilities of the CICS performance analyst.

We haven't gotten as far as CICS yet, and we won't if CICS is at its limit as far as the maximum number of tasks it can accept is concerned, that is, if the number of tasks accepted by CICS for processing is equal to the value defined in the MXT parameter of the SIT or the value to which the initial setting has been changed by the master terminal operator using the CEMT or the CSMT transaction.

It is not unrealistic to have spent one or two seconds getting as far as we have gotten so far. The fact that it is only now that an internal response time would start to be recorded (except in the case of a few third party CICS performance monitors) is the reason why the end-

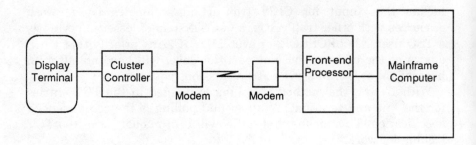

Figure 8-1   Physical path through a typical network.

user is not impressed when told that the computer center is consistently delivering subsecond response times. Figure 8-1 shows the path taken by the data in a typical transaction.

The actual processing of our transaction is uninfluenced by the terminal from which it has been initiated, except in the situation where the TRMPRTY parameter of the TCT is used to assign the transaction a priority value based on the terminal employed.

Having built our screen output in its buffers, CICS can now concern itself with delivering it to our terminal. The first leg of the return journey is from the mainframe to the communications controller. This is also the moment the timer recording the internal response time of the transaction will stop. We can expect our line transmission time to exceed considerably the time taken on the outward journey. If we find ourselves lumbered with a 1200 bits per second data transmission facility, we could find this part of the transaction taking 13 painful seconds to send a full screen's worth of data.

In our example, we have so far only concerned ourselves with a single task. Any delays inherent in the the network design will be compounded should any component be subjected to rates of utilization with which it is unable to cope.

The management of the terminal network has an enormous influence on the overall performance of CICS. The lack of direct control over how it is organized can be a considerable frustration to the performance analyst charged with the well-being of a CICS system. A lot of things that improve overall CICS performance or at least optimize the performance of key resources are outside his or her direct control.

Terminal Control Table Entries

When dealing with the TCT, the prime consideration should *not* be what you code for each TCT entry but *how many* TCT entries you code. Although the introduction of CICS 1.7 has meant streamlined TCTs for VTAM users, I offer the following cautionary tale as a warning to others.

I have come across an installation using the same TCT for production and test CICS systems, although there was literally only a handful of the 100 or so terminals that would want access to both systems. It did have the advantage of making table maintenance much simpler, and it meant that office reorganizations did not have to involve table reassemblies. Unfortunately, this in no way compensated for the waste of storage caused by generating table entries for terminals that would never be used on either CICS system.

To make matters worse, it was also considered a good idea to code entries for each port on every 3274 control unit, regardless of whether there was a terminal plugged into it or not. It was reasoned that some day that there would be a terminal connected so this would save the hassle of regenerating the TCT later by making the changes now.

Again, there were advantages. Some remote users would order terminals or move them around without telling anybody. With this method of TCT maintenance, it didn't matter especially as the company had standardized on IBM 3278 and 3279 model 2s as its preferred screens.

With each TCT entry taking up about half a kilobyte, you can begin to appreciate just how much excess baggage both of these CICS systems were carrying. What's more, I have subsequently found many others guilty of the same crime to some degree or other.

Most installations have quite a number of terminals for which entries have been generated but which are never used — perhaps not as many as in the first case, but they are there just the same.

The Automatic Installation of Terminals

One of the most important facilities that IBM delivered with CICS 1.7 was the "Automatic Installation of Terminals" or autoinstall facility. This was a positive response by IBM to a number of requests made by user groups for such a facility.

Users who have several terminals of the same type need provide CICS with only a single model definition to cover these terminals. When the terminal operator logs on to CICS via VTAM, an appropriate model definition is used to build the necessary control blocks, work areas, etc. needed for the terminal to communicate with CICS, and it is only subsequent to this activity that CICS uses any storage on behalf of the terminal. More importantly, the storage is released when the user logs off.

The sort of installation which will benefit most from autoinstall is the one with a high proportion of transient CICS users: the site which takes its user-base from a large network but has relatively few terminals on-line to CICS at any given moment.

Autoinstall can cause a problem if a large number of users log-on using the facility at the same time. Additional CPU cycles will be used while CICS combines details obtained from VTAM, such as the user's logon-id, with information contained in the appropriate model definition. It uses this information to determine the size and type of the various control blocks, etc. to be associated with this terminal. There will be further increased activity when these storage areas are acquired.

In bad cases this can result in users who are already logged on, experiencing a phenomenon similar to that of someone at the cinema or theater, who having taken his or her seat in good time, is subjected to the disconcerting irritation caused by latecomers arriving after the start of the show.

Don't underestimate the effect of such an activity on a user. Surprisingly often, end-users are much more likely to complain about erratic performance than about response times which are consistently, say, half a second more than has been agreed upon.

The CICS systems programmer has some control over the autoinstall process, and this is provided by the "Autoinstall User Program." This program is invoked when a user logs on off and in its supplied form it matches the characteristics of the terminal used with one of its model definitions.

The logic of this program can be modified or extended, and clearly the case above would benefit greatly by the addition of some user code.

A limit to the number of terminals that will be accepted for autoinstall processing within a set period of time could be maintained in, for example, temporary storage, along with the time of day when autoinstall was last invoked and a running total for the time span. This could help to prevent the system being "swamped" with a surfeit of log-on requests.

The Autoinstall User Program offers a great amount of flexibility, but remember the logic will be invoked at each autoinstall attempt. It is important to temper the needs of the installation with the amount of extra overhead required to support those needs.

VTAM and NCP Considerations

The behavior of a terminal in a VTAM network is controlled by the VTAM or NCP definition that refers to it. There are several parameters that can influence the performance of a given device to the benefit or detriment of other devices in the network. Although, as I have mentioned, the control of VTAM and the NCP is outside the province of many CICS systems programmers, someone in the organization must be aware of the importance of VTAM and NCP parameters and the implications to performance that can be brought about by selecting suboptimal settings.

The NCP

Several NCP parameters influence overall network performance. Since this book is primarily about CICS performance, this look at some of them can, of necessity, only be a brief one.

In particular, there are NCP parameters to restrict the amounts of data flowing between subareas and to regulate the frequency with which data is sent to and received from individual components of the network.

Of particular interest is the value defined in the NCP for MAXOUT. This defines the number of frames that are to be sent before an acknowledgement of their receipt is required. By having MAXOUT set too low, outbound data can be unnecessarily delayed while waiting for this acknowledgement.

The PASSLIM parameter is another that can effect outbound data transmission. It is used to define the number of frames that will be sent by an LU to the control unit at any one time. This prevents any LU from saturating the control unit with data by limiting the number of frames sent, thus effectively splitting the message from the LU into more conveniently sized pieces.

An important NCP parameter specified at the LINE level is the SERVICE parameter. This is used to define the order in which LUs will be polled. By coding some LUs more than once, polling and service can be directed to terminals that require more attention than others, either because of their characteristics or because there is a business requirement for them to receive better service.

Another parameter concerned with polling is the PAUSE parameter, which is also specified in the LINE entry. PAUSE is used to define the minimum length of time between polling cycles. By keeping this at a reasonable level, the time between successive polls can be minimized during periods of low activity. This overhead of additional processor time incurred doing futile work during slack moments needs to be balanced against the amount of increased time in terminals spent waiting to be polled.

It should be pointed out that any benefits that might be bestowed on terminals by way of favorable NCP parameter definitions will also profit those terminals in *all* the VTAM applications they execute.

The TCT

Another cause of the "late theater-goer" phenomenon described in the section on automatic installation of terminals can arise from specifying GMMSG in the TCT entry for VTAM terminals. This causes the CICS "Good morning" message to be displayed when the user logs on.

The effects of this can be intensified if CONNECT=AUTO is specified for several or all of the site's terminals as CICS will try to establish a session with all these terminals when it comes up and then send them the "Good morning" message.

This can all be minimized, however, by limiting the number of concurrent VTAM log-ons for the CICS system. This is done by means of the OPNDLIM parameter of the TCT TYPE=INITIAL macro. The default is 10. Set it lower if you experience problems in this area.

BTAM Considerations

BTAM is functionally inferior to VTAM. It does not allow the user to switch between different CICS systems or to and from TSO as VTAM does. BTAM does require less virtual and real storage to run than VTAM, but generally speaking it does not perform as fast nor as well as VTAM.

Its error recovery routines are nowhere near as comprehensive or as effective as those of VTAM. This often results in a loss of service, particularly to remote users, simply as the result of a little "noise" on the line. This can prove to be equally frustrating to end-user and network controller alike.

As a result, several installations have implemented their own solutions to improve the uptime of their BTAM lines. Many choose to code their own Terminal Error Program (DFHTEP) along with its associated Terminal Error Program Table (DFHTEPT). By supplanting the CICS-supplied DFHTEP and DFHTEPT, they find they are able to prevent their BTAM lines and terminals being placed "out of service" quite so readily.

Others adopt the approach of periodically scanning the TCT, or invoking the master terminal program DFHEMTA, from a timer-driven routine to check for any lines being "out of service." By recording previous activity in temporary storage, they can attempt to put any lines that have dropped "out of service" back "in service."

The overhead of either of these two approaches to the problem must be weighed against the improvements in line availability that they will bring. It should also be borne in mind that these types of solution will only be effective where the problem is a temporary one. Some mechanism needs to be employed to prevent continuous attempts to restore service to hopeless cases. Persistently trying to put a line back "in service" when the modem has just burst into flames is obviously a waste of CPU cycles.

Network Configuration

Although it is unusual for CICS systems programmers in large installations to get involved with the physical aspects of terminal placement and network configuration, many of their brothers and sisters at medium and small shops will be well accustomed to rolling up their sleeves and getting their hands a little dirty.

The planning of a network needs to be based on allowing plenty of room for expansion and growth in the future. Once the initial design has been agreed upon, machinery needs to be put in place to ensure that its performance is regularly reviewed and that additional hardware is phased in carefully rather than coming as a terrible surprise to someone one day.

```
DC    XL1'C2'              WRITE CONTROL COMMAND
DC    XL1'1D'              START FIELD(SF)
DC    XL1'E8'              PROTECTED,INTENSIFIED
DC    XL1'11'              SET BUFFER ADDRESS (SBA)
DC    XL2'405A'            ROW 1 COL 27
DC    CL28'CUSTOMER MASTER FILE ENQUIRY'
DC    XL1'11'              SBA
DC    XL2'C16A'            ROW 2 COL 27
DC    CL28'_____'
DC    XL1'11'              SBA
DC    XL2'C44A'            ROW 4 COL 27
DC    CL22'ENTER CUSTOMER NUMBER:'
DC    XL1'1D'              SF
DC    XL1'D1'              UNPROTECTED,NUMERIC
DC    CL7'.......'
```

Figure 8-2 A typical 3270 data stream.

```
DC    XL1'C2'                WRITE CONTROL COMMAND
DC    XL1'1D'                START FIELD (SF)
DC    XL1'E8'                PROTECTED,INTENSIFIED
DC    XL1'11'                SET BUFFER ADDRESS (SBA)
DC    XL2'405A'              ROW 1 COL 27
DC    CL28'CUSTOMER MASTER FILE ENQUIRY'
DC    XL1'11'                SBA
DC    XL2'C16A'              ROW 2 COL 27
DC    XL1'3C'                REPEAT TO ADDRESS (RA)
DC    XL2'C2C5'              ROW 2 COL 54
DC    CL1' '
DC    XL1'11'                SBA
DC    XL2'C44A'              ROW 4 COL 27
DC    CL22'ENTER CUSTOMER NUMBER:'
DC    XL1'1D'                SF
DC    XL1'D1'                UNPROTECTED,NUMERIC
DC    XL1'3C'                RA
DC    XL2'C4E5'              ROW 4 COL 54
DC    CL1'.'
```

Figure 8-3 A compressed 3270 data stream.

The biggest influences working against a network planner in achieving a balanced network are the two quite different characteristics of printers and display screens. For this reason every effort must be made to separate them as far as practicable. Ideally, this would mean having printers connected to separate control units and lines from those used for display screens.

This can, of course, be quite an expensive solution and many sites elect to place printers at the last available address on the control unit (if they are running under BTAM) or to make sure that the ORDER parameter of the NCP SERVICE macro is coded to ensure less polling is directed at printer terminals (if they are running under VTAM).

It is also important not to overload lines and cluster controllers. There is no point in making sure that every port on a cluster controller has a terminal connected to it if by so doing the controller or line reaches a utilization rate with which the rest of the system cannot cope.

Maximizing the usage of cluster controllers will not, in most cases, optimize performance. Just as it is necessary for DASD to be organized so that high-usage data sets reside on underallocated volumes, so terminals for which there is a requirement for high performance should be placed on dedicated or low-usage lines and controllers.

Data Compression

Compressing output data streams is one way of reducing the amount of data actually sent to a terminal. With 3270 data streams, this is accomplished by looking for characters that are consecutively repeated many times and replacing them with a "repeat to address" sequence in the data stream. Figures 8-2 and 8-3 illustrate how this works.

Obviously, such a strategy will only work when such a pattern of data is likely to occur. There might not be too much to gain if the data stream was, for example, comprised of a lot of text. It is also generally recognized that there is unlikely to be a benefit to using data compression on locally attached display screens, although there is some point in applying it to locally attached terminal printers. In the case of locally attached display screens, the difference between the saving in transmission time of a compressed data stream and the time actually taken to reduce that data stream will in all probability be minimal.

Data streams can be intercepted at CICS global user exit points. The exit will be XZCOUT1 in the module DFHZCB for VTAM users, XTCOUT in the module DFHTCP for BTAM users, and XTCTOUT in the module DFHTCP for TCAM users.

CICS users can write their own exits or they might find one in the public domain if they enquire at their local CICS User Group meeting. Of course, as is true generally, you only get what you pay for and a better answer might be to buy a package from a third-party software vendor. The principal products in today's marketplace are listed in the Appendix.

With the exception of CICS-WINDOWS, these products offer very similar performance and benefits at approximately the same price. In the case of CICS-WINDOWS, the data stream compression facility is a part of a multiple CICS session manager. The price of the product reflects this fact.

Using Basic Mapping Support

The Need for BMS

Basic Mapping Support (BMS) is an important ingredient of most CICS systems. It provides applications programmers with the ability to handle terminal data without needing to know any of the actual physical characteristics of the the device they are dealing with. Its presence in CICS is in keeping with the philosophy of the CICS development team of distancing applications programmers as far as possible from the elements of which they do not require an intimate knowledge.

The applications programmer does need, however, to have a good understanding of how BMS works. By having this understanding, he or she can prevent a great deal of data being unnecessarily transmitted and in so doing play a vital role in improving performance.

BMS Page Building and Message Routing

The BMS page-building capability and the BMS message-routing facility are two powerful commands at the disposal of the CICS programmer, and there are obviously situations for which either or both are ideally suited. Unfortunately, they can also be very heavy on resources.

Page Building. BMS paging uses CICS temporary storage quite extensively. While temporary storage is not the bottleneck in CICS 1.7 that it was in previous releases, it can still be a constraining influence, and its use needs to be carefully considered.

Message Routing. BMS message routing provides a simple and convenient method of delivering a short message to another terminal user. It does, however, need to be used with a great deal of care and consideration. Used thoughtlessly, it can result in hundreds, if not thousands, of messages swamping the network simultaneously. ROUTE=ALL in particular must be used with extreme caution.

BMS Send Map Options

There is a great deal of flexibility built into BMS, which enables users to limit the amounts of data sent. Naturally, to be used effectively they require a little more work on the part of the programmer, but the reductions in line traffic that they can bring about make their use very desirable.

ERASEUP. Most data entry applications are written so that the operator is presented with a "fill the blanks" screen. Usually this screen consists of a number of fields which serve as prompts to the operator. These fields contain constant data and do not change. Adjacent to these fields is an area, sometimes preformatted with full stops or other special characters, which will contain the variable data that the operator keys in.

Once the data has been validated, the operator is presented with the original screen again. The fields designated for the input are reset so that the operator can repeat the cycle.

Rather than send the constant data each time data has to be entered, the programmer can use the ERASEUP option to clear the variable data on either a SEND MAP command or a SEND CONTROL command. ERASEUP clears only the unprotected fields from the screen display, that is the fields designed to receive data, leaving the fields containing constants unchanged. Using ERASEUP, the actual data transmitted is minimal.

MAPONLY and DATAONLY. The vast majority of maps are defined as MODE=INOUT. This means that the output area redefines or overlays the input area. Normally, a map sent to the terminal will consist of a combination of the input and output areas, but this may not be what we want.

If we are designing a data entry transaction, our initial SEND MAP command should use the MAPONLY option. This will set up the initial "template" screen display from which the operator can work. By specifying MAPONLY on the first time through, only the constant data will be sent.

If, on the other hand, our data entry application detects an error at the validation stage, we will probably want to inform the operator of this fact and give him or her the opportunity of correcting it.

Under these circumstances, we could move an error message to an appropriate field and use the SEND MAP command with the DATAONLY option. In this case, the result will be that only variable data is retransmitted.

Summary

In using BMS, the job of the CICS programmer can be greatly simplified. It is quite possible, however, to have an application operating as designed from the point of view of screen presentations but at the expense of considerable extra overhead caused by long terminal transmission times. Extra care and thoughtfulness at the design and development stages will produce savings later on.

9

Monitoring CICS Performance

This chapter looks at the methods and options available to the CICS performance analyst who wants to monitor the performance of a CICS system or systems. It examines how effective the basic CICS-supplied statistics can be in this capacity and goes on to look at the offerings of third-party software suppliers. Finally, there are some suggestions for anyone considering writing their own CICS performance monitor.

The Basic Options

When it comes to monitoring the performance of a CICS system, performance analysts have three basic potential sources of information available to them:

- Use standard CICS-supplied statistics
- Use a software performance monitor
- Write their own routines to extract additional information

Their choice will be determined by the company's willingness (or otherwise) to sink money into a project from which there may not be an obvious and immediate gain. Although any investment in terms of cash or manpower should be proportionate to the importance that the enterprise places on having an efficient CICS system, sadly this is by no means always the case.

All too frequently I hear of installations which demand optimum efficiency from their CICS systems but are not prepared to invest sufficient funds to ensure such demands are met. Such short-sightedness places enormous and unnecessary strain on the poor unfortunate responsible for the well-being of CICS.

In my view, the importance of impressing upon senior management the value of good performance-related tools should be second only to the importance of impressing upon that management the value of oneself.

Having said this, it is also possible to go to the other extreme and to produce a glut of figures and statistics, which by the nature of their very volume obscure the true picture. A one-page summary is much more likely to be read and to consequently pinpoint actual or potential problem areas than a multi-page listing at the actual task level. Moreover, if the person analyzing the data does not have sufficient skill or experience, his or her interpretation may become that of a hypochondriac, and all sorts of nonexistent problems might be imagined.

So let's look at the options, bearing in mind that only you will be able to decide on their suitability for your needs. Running a performance monitor or your own routines will impose an extra overhead in terms of CPU load on your system. This is acknowledged by many third party software vendors who, although they don't highlight the fact, will bury somewhere in their sales literature the increase in CPU time their product will cause. Typically this figure is in the range of 1 to 5% of the total CPU time attributable to CICS, which is not insignificant.

Of course, there is a chance that you might get into a situation where your performance monitor tells you that your only performance problems are caused by your running a performance monitor.

CICS-Supplied Statistics

As you might expect, the quality of CICS-supplied statistics is pretty basic. Most of the figures point to the amount of usage attributable to the main resources such as files, terminals, programs, transactions, storage, etc.

CICS statistics are generated automatically at the end of a CICS run, providing CICS has terminated normally. If the CICS session has not terminated normally, the routines will not be invoked and these shut-down statistics will not be produced.

This fact should be borne in mind should you be accumulating end-of-day statistics to help in a tuning exercise.

Another way of obtaining these statistics is to use the CICS-supplied transaction CSTT. As delivered, the user has two basic options:
• On-request statistics
• Automatic statistics

On Request Statistics

These statistics are generated in response to the transaction CSTT being invoked with the AOR or SOR parameters, as shown in Figure 9-1. The statistics produced are the total counts against the resource or resources since CICS was started up.

The output is routed by default to the transient data queue CSSL. In the CICS-supplied DCTs this queue is in turn associated with an extrapartition data set with the name of MSGUSR.

Automatic Statistics

Automatic statistics are produced in response to CSTT being invoked with the AUT option plus the necessary subparameters. These subparameters consist of the resource to be reported on and the frequency with which CSTT is to action this request. The record counts are reset to zero at the beginning of each time period.

The output is directed to two queues on a flip-flop basis, CSSM and CSSN (don't get this confused with the sign-on transaction of the same name), which in turn are associated with the file names of DFHSTM and DFHSTN, respectively.

The file being used for data collection will automatically switch when it becomes full or it can be forcibly switched by using the CSTT AUT,SWITCH command. A batch program, DFHSTUP, is provided by IBM for the formatting and printing of these files.

CSTT AOR dest

> Send all statistics collected to date to transient data
> destination dest (default CSSL).

CSTT AOC dest

> Send all statistics collected to date to transient data
> destination dest (default CSSL) and reset counters
> to zero.

CSTT SOR dest statstype,DONE

> Send all statistics of type statstype collected to date
> to transient data destination dest (default CSSL) where
> statstype can be one or more of the following:

DUMP	Dump statistics
DYTB	Dynamic Transaction Backout statistics
FILE	File statistics
IRCM	Inter-region Control statistics
JOUR	Journalling Statistics
LINK	Inter-System Communication and Multi-Region Operation statistics
PROG	Transaction and program statistics
STOR	Storage statistics
TASK	Task statistics
TEMP	Temporary storage statistics
TERM	Terminal statistics
TRAN	Transient data statistics

DONE is used to indicate the end of input.

CSTT SOC dest statstype,DONE

> As CSTT SOR etc except that the specified counters
> are also reset to zero.

Figure 9-1   Format of the CSTT command.

Important Statistics

With the possibility of so many different items pertaining to the performance of a CICS run being produced, it becomes difficult to see the wood for the trees. There are many critical indicators, however, that can give a good guide as to how well, or otherwise, a CICS system has behaved. Taking the trouble to check out the following items will prove well worth the effort.

Peak Number of Tasks. This will give you that maximum number of tasks that were in the system at any one time during the relevant period. It can be especially relevant in installations which have service level agreements that define the maximum number of tasks that can be serviced during a defined period of time. It is also important to be able to build a profile showing the transaction rate for given hours of the day.

Number of Times at Maximum Task. This will tell you how often the number of tasks being processed by a CICS system was equal to the figure defined in the MXT parameter of the SIT, which represents the maximum number of tasks that may be present in the system at any one time.

This figure should ideally be zero, and in any case should be quite low. Regularly hitting MXT will show itself in increased response times and is an indication of a CICS system running below its full potential.

One reason for MXT being miscalculated can be the presence of a number of conversational tasks. These can badly distort the true requirement necessary for an optimum MXT setting. IBM ensures that every installation has at least one conversational transaction — CEMT and CESN, for instance.

Maximum Number of Active Tasks Reached. This will tell you the maximum number of active tasks that were being processed at any one time. Note that it is not phrased in quite the same way as the previous item.

I (and I suspect others have too) made the mistake of taking this figure to be the number of times that my CICS system had been processing a number of tasks equal to the figure I had defined for AMXT in my SIT — it is not.

If this figure is less than the figure you have defined in the AMXT parameter of the SIT, your CICS system never got into the situation where the number of active tasks was equal to the AMXT value.

Unfortunately, if this figure is equal to your AMXT value, you can only deduce that the number of active tasks was equal to the AMXT setting *on at least one occasion.* You cannot tell from these statistics exactly how many times that your CICS system was actually in an AMXT situation.

Transaction Class Statistics. If you have used the CMXT parameter of the SIT and the TCLASS parameter of the PCT to divide your transactions into classes, you will get the following statistics for every class that you have defined:

• Maximum number of tasks allowed
• Number of times at maximum task
• Peak number of tasks reached

Maximum number of tasks allowed is the value defined in the CMXT parameter of the SIT for the transaction class in question. Number of times at maximum task is the number of instances when the number of transactions of the class being recorded was equal to the value defined in the CMXT parameter of the SIT for that particular class. Peak number of tasks reached is the maximum number of tasks of a particular class that were being processed at any given time.

If you are using transaction classes to help balance your CICS workload more evenly, these statistics give you a further level of information to help you determine the effectiveness of your actions. You should be able to pinpoint bottlenecks more easily from this additional level of information.

Number of Times Storage Cushion Was Released. This statistic is a record of the number of times that CICS has detected a situation where a GETMAIN request could not be satisfied because of insufficient free virtual storage in the DSA or because the DSA was too fragmented and it has had to use the storage cushion.

The storage cushion is an area of the DSA that CICS sets aside for just such an emergency. Its size is defined in the SCS parameter of the SIT.

If this figure is anything other than zero or a very low figure, it is an obvious indication of stress and the need to identify the cause of the constraint.

Number of Times Storage Request Was Queued. This can be a further indication of stress. It is a record of the number of times that CICS could not meet a storage request.

Number of Times Storage Queue Was Established. A value against this statistic of anything other than zero or a very low figure will also point to a troubled system. This figure plus the the number of times that the storage cushion was released will be the number of times that CICS posted a "short on storage" condition (CSASOSI in CSA equal to X'01').

Peak Number of Requests in Storage Queue. This records the maximum number of tasks waiting for storage at any given time. It illustrates the depth of any stress problem.

Times Program Called by Transaction. This is one of the statistics available for CICS transactions. It is simply a record of the amount of usage of programs associated with PCT entries. As not every program is associated with a transaction, it is not a comprehensive record of all program activity.

Nevertheless, it can provide a good basis for the analysis of trends if these figures are accumulated regularly over a reasonable period of time. It will also pinpoint any unused transactions in your system, if you have any.

Times Transaction Was Stall-Purged. This is probably not of too much use at the transaction level. It is the number of times that a transaction was purged from the system because the system was under severe stress. As most stress situations are caused by a general lack of storage rather than the running of particular transactions, it is probable that this figure will only really indicate how many times a transaction was unfortunate enough to be purged, i.e., it just happened to be in the system at the wrong time. The overall total for all transactions is, however, again an important indicator of a virtual storage-constrained system.

Times Transaction Restarted. This will tell you how many time a transaction that was defined in the PCT with the RESTART=YES option was restarted after an abend. Normally these are transactions that have failed during DL/I processing because of a program isolation deadlock.

If this figure is very high, your system is incurring a considerable overhead in performing these restarts. Circumventing the cause of the deadlocks by application redesign or even the introduction of some manual system of control should be seriously considered.

Times Program Used. This reveals how many times a program or map was used by CICS. This figure should be captured over a reasonably long period of time and used, in conjunction with data concerning its size, to determine whether the program or map is a suitable candidate to be made resident or not.

Times Program Fetched. The number of times that a program has been fetched refers to the number of times that a nonresident program had to be loaded into the DSA from the library on disk. As the number of program compressions is not recorded by CICS, this is the best guide available short of investing in third-party software.

The ratio of times fetched to times used is an indication of how quickly the DSA is being used up and how often the subsequent program compressions are occurring.

Number of Storage Dumps. The number of storage dumps is not a direct indication of performance problems, although there is, of course, increased system activity when they are produced. Making sure that those concerned are fully aware of any dumps produced and putting pressure on those responsible to ensure their speedy resolution should have some influence on future performance.

Number of Terminal Input and Output Messages. This is the most important measure of an individual terminal's activity. Where a terminal network has more than one line or control unit servicing terminals at the same physical location, it may well be possible to balance the workload more evenly on the basis of these figures taken over a period of time. Alternatively, these figures could provide the justification for increased expenditure on lines and/or control units.

These figures will also pinpoint any terminals that are never used and which can be removed from the TCT saving around 500 bytes per terminal.

Number of Terminal Transmission Errors. To be of any use, there must be a predetermined threshold against which this figure can be compared. Although ensuring a low transmission error count is beyond the responsibility of most performance analysts, it remains his or her duty to inform the person responsible of any shortcomings in this area.

The overhead caused by transmission error recovery routines should not be overlooked. Making sure that the relevant hardware is in the best of condition will ensure that this unproductive CPU time is kept to a minimum.

Maximum Number of RPLs Posted. This statistic concerns VTAM terminals and represents the maximum number of RPLs that have been posted by VTAM for any single dispatch of CICS terminal control. It should be used in conjunction with the next statistic (number of times reached maximum) and compared with the RAPOOL value defined in the SIT.

Number of Times Reached Maximum. This figure reflects the suitability (or otherwise) of the RAPOOL parameter. A value of zero would probably indicate that too many VTAM receive-any buffers have been allocated and could be reduced by lowering the RAPOOL value.

VTAM Short-on-Storage Count. A large figure against this statistic is indicative of a VTAM problem rather than a CICS one. CICS will automatically retry the failing request. VTAM going short on storage can be prevented or reduced by increasing VTAM buffers.

VSAM File Requests. VSAM file requests are broken down into the different categories of file access:

• GETs
• GETs for UPDATE
• BROWSEs
• ADDs
• UPDATEs
• DELETEs

These statistics reflect the amount of logical I/O activity, not the amount of physical I/O. This should be kept in mind if you want to use these figures to help in the physical placement of data sets across your available DASD. This is because sometimes CICS can satisfy a read request from existing buffers. In this case an I/O is still recorded in these statistics even though no physical activity has taken place.

These figures, if collected over a reasonable period of time, will provide a good basis for determining whether a file is a suitable candidate for LSR or not.

Wait-on-Strings Total. This is a good guide to how effective your choice of value for the STRNO parameter for this data set is. A small percentage of all file requests should incur a wait-on-string unless you have bags of virtual storage to play with. As a rough guide, most experts would quote a figure of 5%.

If the wait-on-strings total for any data set is zero, the likelihood is that you are allocating buffers to that data set which are never used and are therefore wasted.

If your system is short of virtual storage, consider reducing the STRNO value until you get to the point where 5% of your file requests are waiting for strings.

If more than 5% of your file requests are waiting for strings and there is insufficient virtual storage for you to increase the STRNO value, consider reducing MXT or CMXT so that the task waits earlier in its task life.

Wait-on-Strings Highest. This records the maximum number of file requests that were waiting at any one time because of insufficient strings. It is an indication of the depth of the problem concerning the shortage of strings.

Highest Number of Requests Waited for Buffer (LSR Files Only). This statistic records the maximum number of file requests against the data set that were waiting at any one time because no buffers of the appropriate size were available. This value should be very low, otherwise you are defeating the purpose of using LSR buffers.

This figure needs to be compared with the next statistic — total number of requests waited for buffer — to determine whether any problem is caused by a heavy loading on the CICS system at one particular time or whether the data set is waiting for buffers consistently throughout the day.

Total Number of Requests Waited for Buffers (LSR Files Only). This is a record of the total number of file requests made against a data set, which could not be immediately satisfied because of a lack of buffers of the appropriate size.

In some instances it will be found that the problem is caused by an inequitable distribution of buffers for certain buffer sizes. This shows itself when all the data sets of certain CISIZEs are never waiting for buffers, while the frequency of buffer waits for data sets of other CISIZEs is quite high.

Number of Successful Look-Asides (LSR Files Only). The number of successful look-asides is the number of read requests that CICS was able to satisfy because the buffer was already in virtual storage. This is obviously a very desirable state of affairs, as it means that no physical I/O has had to be initiated.

A total figure is given for each buffer size, and in this way you can see what effect increasing or decreasing the number of buffers for any one buffer size has on the total number of successful look-asides. Unfortunately, being able to satisfy a read request from a buffer already in virtual storage also depends on many site-dependent variables — the actual transaction mix and the number of active tasks are both key factors.

CICS Software Performance Monitors

There is a wide variety of CICS performance monitors available to help users tune their systems. They range in capability from the most basic, which provide little more than a convenient display of some of the more important control blocks, to those that can control many CICS systems from a single terminal and sound the alarm bells should predetermined performance thresholds be exceeded.

I am a great believer in the adage "you get what you pay for." While this may sound like an oversimplification of the dilemma facing CICS performance analysts, it is as well to be reminded of it. While the marketing of mainframe computer software is a pretty competitive business, profit margins are finely honed, and true bargains are very few and far between.

The following list of CICS software performance monitors, although comprehensive, is not a definitive buyer's guide. While it would have proved very interesting to have taken each of these products and run them for a month or so in the same environment to see just how they compared, this naturally proved impossible.

The comments made alongside the following products are intended purely as a guide to any prospective buyers of CICS monitors. They are drawn from a combination of the vendor's own publicity, independent user's experiences, and the author's own experiences.

ADR/LOOK

The CICS Monitor Facility of ADR/LOOK is only a part of a much wider reaching performance tool. The product gives a large number of useful displays regarding the performance of a CICS system showing the current status and total usage by transaction, file, and program. Detailed analysis of programs created by ADR's own application generator, ADR/IDEAL, are available but there is no similar support for any of the other application generators. ADR/LOOK can be run from a different MVS address space or VSE partition than the CICS system it is monitoring.

BEST/1-MVS

The CICS Feature of BEST/1-MVS is again just a part of a much bigger product. It is a batch-only product and only available under MVS. It takes CMF data and produces transaction performance information in both a detailed and summarized form. Resource utilization is broken down by system component usage. The product can be used to build models of different CICS systems for analysis and as an aid to capacity planning.

BIMODIS

BIMODIS is a fairly inexpensive yet effective product, which can be used to obtain useful displays of what is currently going on in CICS and the operating system. There are versions available for both VSE and MVS, although it would appear that the VSE version has a fuller repertoire and gives the user an insight into the major VSE control blocks and key DL/I information. The manual that accompanies BIMODIS has been well received by its users — it contains general information on CICS and the operating system and suggests ways in which BIMODIS can be used to help solve any problems.

CA-JARS/CICS

CA-JARS/CICS is primarily a data collection and reporting product with only a limited on-line display facility and was conceived originally as a job accounting tool. Data is grouped by transaction, terminal, or file and the output can be in the form of system use reports, resource utilization graphs, or user-defined reports using the powerful report generator. Backed by the world's largest third-party software vendor, reliability is, of course, not a problem.

CICS MANAGER

CICS MANAGER is a fairly recent newcomer to the scene, although Boole and Babbage have considerable experience in producing good performance tools. There are VSE and MVS versions available, and the product can be run from outside CICS. It has a hierarchical menu design and good on-line help facilities. CICS MANAGER monitors the CICS region or partition, ensuring that predefined service levels are being met. If this is not so, it can take automatic corrective action or it can issue a warning to the operator.

CICS MANAGER has good batch reporting capabilities and an interface to the statistical analysis tool, MICS. As well as DL/I, there is support for ADABAS, ADR/DATACOM, and IDMS. Applications written in GENER/OL, ADR/IDEAL, NATURAL, and UFO are also catered for.

CICSPARS

CICSPARS is for VSE and MVS users running releases of CICS prior to 1.7. It collects CICS performance data and reports on it. It covers all the main areas critical to good performance including response times, transaction rates, paging rates, virtual and real storage utilization. The on-line displays are a bit limited, and there are of course no interfaces with any third-party software. GPAR or DOS/GPAR is needed to run the reports.

CICSPARS/MVS and CICSPARS/VSE

CICSPARS/MVS and CICSPARS/VSE are a vast improvement on CICSPARS and the other previous IBM offering PAII, although needing to go quite a bit further to catch up with the products from the leading independent software companies. The on-line displays of resource consumption are good, and there is an Alert Monitor, which sounds an audible alarm if user-defined limits on certain resources are exceeded. Graphics are supported through GDDM.

EPILOG 1000 FOR CICS

EPILOG 1000 FOR CICS is meant as a batch reporting facility for OMEGAMON/CICS. There are VSE and MVS versions and it comes with a conversion utility to allow CMF data to be input. Information can be collected at the transaction level across multiple regions or partitions and on different CPUs. EPILOG 1000 FOR CICS supports DB2 data bases.

ESRA/CICS

ESRA/CICS is a monitor with built-in intelligence. When it identifies a response time problem, it springs into action and invokes its degradation analysis and resource utilization routines automatically producing a hardcopy output of its findings. Response time is broken down into CPU utilization, paging, I/O, CICS services, and time spent queuing for resources. ESRA/CICS is for CICS/OS systems only.

EXPLORE/CICS

EXPLORE/CICS can be run from its own partition or address space. It has a good on-line help facility and a threshold monitoring capability with operator alert. In addition, when it detects that a threshold target has been reached, it can be set to execute automatically a set of EXPLORE/CICS commands in order to extract further information to help solve the problem. It can be set up to monitor certain CICS resources and automatically refresh the display after a user-defined time interval. Batch reporting can be in the form of reports or histograms.

MICS/CICS

MICS/CICS is just a part of a much bigger performance analysis tool for MVS users. It does not have its own data capture mechanism but relies on data from PAII, CMF, or THE MONITOR FOR CICS as its input. It is a batch reporting package and produces reports about CICS service levels concentrating on system availability, transaction throughput, resource usage, forecasting, transaction life cycles, and profile analysis.

The Monitor for CICS

Landmark Systems Corporation has concentrated most of its resources on this one product, which has had considerable success in recent years. It seems to have applied equal importance to on-line monitoring and batch reporting capabilities in addition to making the product easy to use. The Activity Monitor provides an on-line display of currently active tasks, while the Graphic Monitor traces up to 26 user-defined elements and displays up to 20 of these from one display. The other key components comprise a Summary Display, Collection Analysis, a Storage Monitor, and a useful application diagnosis and debugging tool Supertrace.

Part of the success of Landmark Systems is due to their willingness to get "into bed" with other independent software vendors. This allows them to provide interfaces to and support for most of the leading data base management systems (DL/I, DB2, ADABAS, MILLENIUM, SQL/DS, IDMS, DATACOM/DB, and TOTAL) and application generators (ADR/IDEAL, MANTIS, GENER/OL, UFO, DMS, and NATURAL).

OMEGAMON/CICS

This was once the undisputed market leader among CICS performance products. VSE and MVS versions are available, which can be run from a separate partition or region. It is an on-line monitor, although a batch reporting capability can be added through EPILOG/1000. The power of the product is so great that it has been criticized for having too many commands and subcommands! OMEGAMON/CICS has a comprehensive help facility and an on-line tutorial. It has an Alert Monitor, which can be set to sound an alarm when any of a number of user-defined thresholds has been exceeded. Among the many areas encompassed by the product are task degradation, CICS paging problems, task storage violations, VSAM bottlenecks, enqueue bottlenecks, dynamic storage fragmentation, short-on-storage occurrences, and system stalls. Through its newsletter, educational courses, and participation in many other activities, Candle has built up a reputation as a leading center of competence in performance-related matters.

PEEKCSA

I'm sure even the people at MacKinney Systems won't mind me saying that this is not the most sophisticated of all the performance tools in this chapter. The product is basically a series of on-line displays showing current CICS resource activity and usage. With a purchase price of less than $700 or with a one-year lease at less than $300, it does, however, represent excellent value for the money. There are VSE and MVS versions available, with the VSE version slightly richer in function thanks to a display showing system statistics or the console. Both versions have a storage display and alter facility.

PILOT/CICS

I have included this product mainly for the concept which it employs. It is a PC-based CICS performance analyzer, which takes downloaded data and formats it using the power and flexibility of LOTUS 1-2-3. In addition to reporting, PILOT/CICS is also capable of tracking, forecasting, "what-if" analysis, and modeling. PILOT/CICS provides the performance analyst with a much more convenient environment in which to work while at the same time lessening the burden on the mainframe CPU.

RTA/CICS

RTA/CICS is designed to run with one or more of the other members of Candle's CICS performance monitor family. RTA stands for Response Time Analyzer, which is precisely what it is. The data can be grouped by user-defined transaction-related criteria and analyzed by time interval or by specific times of day. Both MVS and VSE versions are available and, in common with other Candle products, there are on-line help and tutorial facilities.

SNOOP FOR CICS

SNOOP FOR CICS provides the user with on-line displays of CICS resources. It helps to identify performance bottlenecks in particular by looking at VSAM usage and string contention. It can also find and display all CICS table entries. There are VSE and MVS versions available.

STROBE/CICS Performance Measurement

This is an MVS-only tool, which analyzes CICS CPU utilization and data base activity. It can be used to identify sections of code that use a lot of CPU time and break it down by CICS and MVS activity (SVCs, I/O modules, etc.). Data base activity can be separated by I/O usage, CPU usage, and CPU wait time. The user can also see the amount of DASD I/O for each cylinder.

System Accounting (REACT)

REACT is the CICS monitoring component of the more extensive VSE job accounting and performance monitoring tool SYSTEM ACCOUNTING. In on-line use, it gives a dynamic snapshot of CICS operation, while longer-term analysis is provided by its historical reporting facilities. Users can home in on problems by way of a series of menus, moving from general displays to a more specific level of detail. User-defined thresholds can be preset to trigger audible and visual warnings. REACT has its own data collection mechanism to avoid the overhead of CMF. Recent data can be held on a VSAM file and displayed in the same format as output from the dynamic monitor.

Writing Your Own Routines to Monitor CICS Performance

It would be surprising if any of the products mentioned so far in this chapter used any techniques not available to the ordinary systems programmer. Given sufficient knowledge of CICS internals, there is no reason why an installation should not reproduce any of the facilities of these products using its own manpower and resources.

But would this be wise? Is it a sensible use of staff and CPU time? The answer is "it depends." It depends on the size of the project. It depends on the level of knowledge of the staff who are going to work on the project. It depends on the comparative cost of a similar piece of software from an independent software vendor.

There should be very little trouble in generating enthusiasm for the project from an individual or a team. Most systems programmers would positively welcome such an opportunity to roll up their sleeves and do "some real work." What may be more of a problem is getting the same response when it comes to maintaining the software and to migrating it to future releases of CICS or perhaps the operating system. If the writer of the software has been too clever, you may find that a software upgrade renders his or her efforts obsolete and most of the work has to be discarded.

There are obvious advantages of having custom-built software. Writing your own performance monitoring routines allows you to concentrate on what you feel is important in respect to your own unique circumstances. Items that have little or no relevance can be ignored, leaving reports and screen displays uncluttered. In this way you are left with information that gets right to the point.

Unfortunately, developing software to match that of the leading independent suppliers would prove prohibitively expensive. What's more, you would largely be "reinventing" the wheel. You should be content with doing little more than displaying CICS statistics in real time rather than waiting for CICS shutdown. This is fairly easily accomplished and lends itself very well as an exercise to teach someone the rudiments of CICS internals.

Some Hints on Coding Your Own Routines

I have said that it is simple to write a routine to extract CICS statistics and display them on a terminal — and it is, providing you know where to find them. The accumulators for all the systemwide statistics used in CICS shutdown statistics or by the CSTT transaction are maintained in the CSA. Figure 9-2 shows some of the most important control blocks that are to be found in the CSA.

CSAKCMTA	Peak number of tasks
CSAKCMTC	Number of times at MAXTASK
CSAMAXTC	Maximum number of active tasks reached
CSAMXT1	Class 1 maximum tasks
CSAMXT1C	Class 1 current tasks
CSAMXT11	Class 1 maximum tasks reached
CSAMXT1M	Class 1 number of times maximum tasks reached
CSAMXT1A	Class 1 active tasks count
CSAMXT2	Class 2 maximum tasks
CSAMXT2C	Class 2 current tasks
CSAMXT2R	Class 2 maximum tasks reached
CSAMXT2M	Class 2 number of times maximum tasks reached
CSAMXT2A	Class 2 active task count
.	
.	and similarly for classes 3-9
.	
CSAMXTA	Class 10 maximum tasks
CSAMXTAC	Class 10 current tasks
CSAMXTAR	Class 10 maximum tasks reached
CSAMXTAM	Class 10 number of times maximum tasks reached
CSAMXTAA	Class 10 active task count
CSASCCR	No of times storage cushion realeased
CSASCRQ	No of times storage request was queued
CSASCQZ	No of times storage queue was established
CSASCMQ	Peak number of requests in storage queue

Figure 9-2   Some useful control blocks in CSA.

How Monitors Are Used in Practice

A very comprehensive survey into how CICS performance monitors are used and what determines their selection in the first place was undertaken by Xephon in 1988. The survey was able to draw on the experiences of users all over the world by sending a questionnaire to the subscribers of CICS Update, which reaches over 3000 installations in 57 different countries. The survey concentrated on the six leading products, namely ADR/LOOK, CICS MANAGER, CICSPARS/MVS (or VSE), EXPLORE/CICS, THE MONITOR FOR CICS, and OMEGAMON/CICS.

CICS performance monitors, in their present form, have only been available since the early eighties but have managed to establish a very strong following in this time. Many sites expressed the feeling that they couldn't operate without them thus illustrating their transition from luxury to necessity. They are not, however, seen as an immediate requirement for new installations. Most shops wait a few years after initially installing CICS before putting in a performance monitor and then often as the result of finding themselves faced with a string of performance problems which they cannot easily untangle.

Furthermore, performance monitors remain largely the tools of systems programmers despite the efforts of the vendors of these products to broaden their appeal and to extend their usage to other areas, particularly the Help Desk, Operations, and the Development Centre. There was a fair amount of evidence to suggest that a great deal of inter-departmental rivalry exists in today's DP shops. Several instances were recorded of errant application programming logic causing some sort of performance problem but where development staff had not been encouraged to use monitoring software. As a result, many problems did not come to light as soon as they should have done. If these applications could have been put under the same sort of close scrutiny in development that they were subjected to in production, the cost of unraveling their shortcomings would have been far less.

General Uses

A great deal was made of the importance of having so much relevant information available from a single source and literally at one's fingertips. Some of those surveyed described how easy it was, using a performance monitor, to highlight a problem, make an appropriate adjustment, and measure the effects of any change. Generally it was in the following spheres of CICS performance where the products surveyed were most commonly used although the full range of uses they were put to was far more extensive.

Identifying Waits

A number of installations saw the ability to identify where and for how long a transaction waited during its lifetime as giving them an important insight into examining CICS performance problems. While some waiting is unavoidable, being able to pinpoint those areas where this is being carried to excess will greatly assist in tuning the application and will give some idea of the size of any benefit likely to be achieved.

Balancing Loads

Sharing resources is fundamental to the whole design of CICS and therefore a degree of contention is to be expected. The commonest areas of contention are likely to be on DASD volumes, DASD channels, terminal control units, communications lines, and the CPU. Some resources, however, experience a disproportionate amount of contention caused by an uneven distribution of the workload. While the basic CICS statistics contain sufficient information to give the CICS tuner a solid basis on which to balance these loads, the extra detail available from a good monitor will greatly simplify the task, especially if multiple CICS systems are involved.

Peak Usage

There can be few, if any, installations that do not have surges in their CICS workloads from 11.00 am to midday and again from 4.00 pm to 5.00 pm, and obviously non-important work, which could have an adverse impact on overall CICS performance, should not be scheduled for these times. A more detailed picture of the peaks and troughs taken over a month, for example, will enable other periods where CICS is also susceptible to interference from other work to be spotted.

Transaction Loops

Most installations will have experienced the frustration caused by not being able to cancel a looping transaction necessitating a restart of CICS. Fortunately, most major monitors nowadays have the capability of being run from outside the CICS address space or partition and, as such, can be used to cancel any rogue transactions without seriously affecting other applications.

VSAM

Many of the sites surveyed showed a keen interest in monitoring the number of times CICS was waiting for VSAM strings for given data sets — perhaps to the point of becoming unhealthily obsessed with their complete elimination. A certain amount of waiting for strings is tolerable in CICS — around 5% of all file requests is a reasonable figure to aim for — and can, under certain circumstances, be positively good for a CICS system. A figure over 10% starts to become harmful and steps should be taken to reduce this number. Applications holding on to strings longer than absolutely necessary can cause needless performance problems but fortunately they can be easily identified by the leading monitors and eventually eliminated from the system.

There was also a few cases reported of applications trying to perform a VSAM DELETE or UPDATE following a BROWSE which had not been ended by the application. To accomplish this, CICS needs two strings — one for the BROWSE and one for the DELETE or UPDATE. If only one string is available, a deadlock is encountered. Here again, monitoring tools were able to identify the problem and provide a means for a temporary circumvention.

Another facet of VSAM performance handled well by performance monitors is the recording of Control Interval (CI) and Control Area (CA) splits. While CI splits will probably be tolerable in most systems, CA splits can degrade a system substantially and are best avoided. Moreover, a CA split requires an additional string for the data set involved. The number of CI and CA splits can be deduced without anything fancier than an IDCAMS LISTCAT listing. Most systems programmers, however, prefer to get this information through a simple-to read-screen display.

Single Transactions

There were many shops in the survey who had built up clear analyses of the different transactions they were running. They were able to break down transactions by the amount of resource usage and the amount of time waiting for resources. In addition to being able to pinpoint bottlenecks in the system; by comparing the profiles they had built up of similar transactions, any substantial deviation from the norm could be recognized and made a suitable candidate for further investigation.

Program Compressions

When CICS performs a program compression, considerable extra overhead is incurred. Standard CICS statistics only allow a user to estimate the frequency with which they have occurred. The latest tools are able to reveal exactly how often program compressions are occurring and how much they are hurting a system.

Storage Allocations

For many, estimating the size of the DSA, GETVIS, or OSCOR is something of a lottery. One of the most frequently used tools for effectively calculating appropriate sizes is the 'wet finger'. A lot of sites start with a 'good guess' and increase it if they hit problems. Over allocating storage often goes undetected. Many of those surveyed found they were able to be more accurate after using a performance monitor.

Specific Uses

The following are some examples of how performance monitors actually helped respondents in the survey to resolve problems. These examples are not contrived nor have they been specifically selected to highlight the capabilities of any single product. In some cases, the problems could have been resolved using more basic methods. These examples do, however, illustrate the wide scope of the tools employed.

Case 1. A VSE installation experiencing GETVIS shortages and fragmentation was able to isolate the cause to a COBOL program using CURRENT- DATE and CURRENT-TIME.

Case 2. A site with IMS/DB data bases discovered that the enqueue pool was getting exhausted by a program that wasn't issuing syncpoints often enough.

Case 3. The problem of an excessively high number of EXCPs to a single VSAM file was attributed to a program performing a skip sequential read from the beginning of a file.

Case 4. Two days away from the scheduled live implementation of a major insurance system response times were 17 seconds. During those two days PSB pool utilization, temporary storage strings, and the number of program loads were examined. As a result of the findings and subsequent tuning, sub-second response was achieved.

Case 5. A large VTAM installation was able to satisfy its management that poor response times were not caused by CICS but by the network resources.

Case 6. A site monitoring the number of EXCPs per I/O request discovered a heavily-used VSAM cluster had unnecessarily being defined with a SHAREOPTION of 4. The number of EXCPs was cut drastically when the cluster was redefined using a better SHAREOPTION.

Case 7. An application with excessively long input message lengths was referred to the development team, who redesigned the application and dramatically reduced the amount of screen data transmitted.

Case 8. An MVS installation reported that it had used IBM guidelines to calculate the amount of OSCOR. When it had reviewed this calculation using a monitor, it was able to trim 1.3 Mb from the amount of storage previously allocated.

Case 9. A display of the Page Allocation Map revealed that areas of the isolated subpool were not being released when they were finished with. A third-party software package was found to be at fault.

Case 10. A heavy VSAM user was able to reduce the number of strings allocated for several files after examining the high water mark of string usage.

Case 11. A NATURAL user was able to alleviate a temporary storage bottleneck by changing the NATURAL parameters FSIZE and ESIZE. In this case, response times were trimmed by 40%.

Case 12. Another site experiencing problems with temporary storage analyzed the queues and found items created by the VS COBOL II formatted dump option. Recompiling these programs with the NOF-DUMP option proved an effective answer in this situation.

Case 13. A VSAM installation was able to see at a glance that there were insufficient buffers in the LSR pool for a particular CI size.

Site 14. A VSE shop was encouraged to migrate to CICS 1.7 to make use of multiple temporary storage strings after seeing how heavily the temporary storage data set was used.

Conclusion

The above examples illustrate some crisis situations and some cases where the actual impact is much less. Small problems have an unfortunate habit of becoming larger problems if left to go unchecked possibly precipitating a premature hardware upgrade. There was more than a little evidence in the survey to suggest that the combination of rich functionality and ease of use present in modern performance monitors are a positive spur to systems programmers and performance analysts in their duties.

10

How to Improve Performance

This chapter looks at the various options open to the CICS performance analyst and discusses some of the typical trade-offs that have
to be made in ensuring that performance objectives are met.

A Methodology

Having looked at the issues relating to CICS performance at a
detailed level in the previous chapters, I should now like to stand
back a little and describe a generalized methodology for tackling performance problems. Some of the following advice is not specific to the
CICS environment but is nonetheless still relevant. I should like to
emphasize that these guidelines are not intended to be rigidly applied. They are intentionally flexible and offer sufficient scope to be
supplemented and tailored according to the individual's needs.

   Learning about performance is a continuous activity. Sure enough,
just when you think you have the subject mastered, along comes an

innovation that turns your cozy view of things upside down. Hardware and software evolve so rapidly that a continual reassessment of the major issues should be undertaken in the light of new developments. In computer technology especially, you cannot afford to stand still for a moment.

Take, for example, what I would personally call the early days of computing, when programs had to be written so that they could be loaded into the limited amount of storage available. In extreme cases, elaborate overlay structures had to be designed in order for a program to fit within the confines allowed to it. The advent of virtual storage freed the applications programmer from this restraint and, while universally welcomed, gave us something new to worry about — paging.

And so it goes on — we come up against a problem, we think about it, we tackle the problem, the problem is solved, another problem appears.

Performance problems occur when an installation is no longer able to meet its service level agreements in full. Running below optimum levels in terms of resource utilization, while undesirable, is not in itself a problem, providing that the end-user is receiving adequate response. A performance problem can only be said to exist if the computer center is unable to deliver performance equal to or better than predefined service objectives.

So, what are the alternatives open to someone confronted by users demanding faster response times? Faced with CICS performance problems, he or she can choose to make matters better by:

1. Adding more hardware or software
2. Improving CICS performance at the expense of other concurrent work
3. Tuning CICS by redistributing resources
4. Renegotiating service level agreements

If the service level agreements have been the subject of vigorous debate prior to their acceptance, and this is usually the case, the last option is unlikely to meet with any degree of success. I have included it because *everything* should be considered at the initial stage, even if it can be dismissed at once. This leaves us with the choice of whether to beg, steal, or borrow.

$AVE/IO   Main Frame Software Products Corporation,
               1 Hollis Street, Suite B12, Weelesley,
               MA 02181, USA
               Telephone: (617) 239 0288.

               Uses its own routines to ensure that the
               heaviest-used data set records are kept in
               storage and thus reduces file I/O activity
               and contetion.

CATS   Fischer International Systems Corporation,
               4073 Mercantile Avenue, Naples,
               FL 33942, USA
               Telephone: (813) 643 1500.

               CICS Accelerated Transaction Scheduler
               reduces the number of accesses to CICS
               program libraries and improves internal
               CICS scheduling.

FETCH   Axios Products Incorporated, 1455
               Veterans Highway, Hauppauge,
               NY 11788-4836, USA
               Telephone: (516) 348 1900.

               Improves CICS performance by using its
               own multi-thread program loader.

Figure 10-1 Third-party software products that improve CICS performance.

Begging

Getting the DP manager to increase expenditure on hardware or software to improve the performance of your CICS system needs to be approached diplomatically — the degree of diplomacy being in direct proportion to the amount of money required. He or she will not appreciate a request for a CPU upgrade just after the annual budget plans have been agreed upon and finalized.

It is not an easy thing to predict accurately the impact that a bought solution will bring. Believe it or not, salesmen have been known to bend the truth a little when it comes to making claims about the amount of improvement their products will give.

As well as the data compression packages mentioned in Chapter Eight, Figure 10-1 shows some other CICS add-on software packages which could improve CICS performance.

It is obviously better — and more likely to have the desired effect — if a product is installed not because a glossy advertisement has caught somebody's eye, but because it will provide the solution to an already defined problem.

One big advantage of a software, as opposed to a hardware, solution, is that the package can be installed on a test CICS system under the supplier's trial period facility and extensively tested in circumstances under which it will eventually be used in anger. If, at the end of this time, it fails to measure up, it can be deinstalled without incurring any direct financial outlay.

It should be kept in mind, however, that hardware upgrades can provide the scope for improvements of a much more spectacular and dramatic nature. As hardware is not so easily installed, greater consideration should be given to it as a solution to performance problems. On the other hand, because of its very nature, performance data on hardware tends to be much more comprehensive and reliable. It is also more predictable.

Hardware improvements should be confined to removing identified bottlenecks. There is obviously no point in installing a more powerful CPU if your main performance problems are caused by your telecommunications lines being too slow and too few.

Stealing

While the word "stealing" implies an amount of dishonesty and stealth in its literal use, I use it here in the sense of benefiting one entity at the expense of taking from another. "Stealing" in this chapter means taking away with the full knowledge and, hopefully, cooperation of the owner.

In MVS this could be by increasing the number of pages used in storage isolation or by a reappraisal of the performance groups in effect.

In VSE, this could be achieved by changing partitions' priorities, altering storage allocations, or by using the TPBAL command.

Both operating systems can be adjusted to permit fewer batch jobs running at the same time as CICS.

It is also possible that a more even distribution of files across DASD and terminals across lines and control units, if undertaken with the best interests of your CICS system in mind, will have an adverse effect on your other workloads. It is important that all interested parties are allowed to participate in the dialogue that hopefully precedes these types of action.

An interesting observation I have made at several sites is that in a really desperate "back-to-the-wall" situation, it is the test CICS system that suffers. A curious decision when you consider that test CICS users (i.e., the application development group) are often among the highest paid employees in the company.

Borrowing

Borrowing is another way to describe tuning, for that is, in essence, what tuning is all about. Having identified a resource that is overcommitted, the pressure is relieved by transferring some of the burden by the increased commitment of another resource.

"Making trade-offs" is the whole essence of performance tuning, and the art of good performance tuning is making the right trade-offs. The following examples illustrate some of the actions that might be taken by a CICS tuner and the consequences that might result.

File I/O Buffers.   Reducing file I/O buffers will correspondingly lighten the load on both virtual and real storage but at the expense of increasing disk I/O activity.

Resident Programs.   Making programs resident (i.e., defining them in the PPT as RES=YES) will reduce disk I/O and the loading of programs and maps, which under CICS is a serial operation, and so any other task requiring that a file be loaded must wait for any prior requests for this facility to complete. This is achieved at the expense of increasing virtual and real storage demands.

DL/I Threads. With DL/I data bases, the DLTHRED parameter in the SIT can be used to control the amount of concurrent DL/I activity. If it is set too low, virtual and real storage demands will probably be reduced but at the expense of increasing the likelihood of tasks waiting.

Page Size. Setting the CICS page size at 2048 instead of 4096 in the SIT will have the effect of reducing the DSA because its packing density will be better but at the risk of increasing paging.

Auxiliary or Main Temporary Storage. Deciding whether to use main or auxiliary temporary storage is a choice between using more real storage (main) or increasing disk I/O activity (auxiliary).

Transaction Priorities. Finally, CICS provides the opportunity of improving the performance of one task at the expense of another. This is accomplished either by using the TCLASS parameter of the PCT in conjunction with the CMXT parameter of the SIT or by a combination of OPPRTY (from the SNT), TRMPRTY (from the TCT), and TRNPRTY (from the PCT).

What Not to Do

As with any methodology, some attention must be given to things that should *not* be done and are to be avoided. There are a few aspects relating to CICS performance that fall into this category, and they have been highlighted in this chapter since they mainly concern commonly held misconceptions, which, however well-intentioned could restrict the maximum potential of a system ever being reached.

Magic Answers. Don't look for magic answers to CICS performance problems. Quite simply, there aren't any. There are no special values to any parameters that will transform your CICS system overnight from a tortoise to a hare. It is not uncommon to find that values considered to be effective at one shop have quite a different effect when used somewhere else.

This can occur on very similar systems running the same types of applications. It cannot be stressed enough that each parameter must be evaluated in the context of the unique environment in which it is to be used.

CICS Parameters. Although there is an obvious temptation to do so, do *not* go back to the CICS Parameters chapter and modify all your CICS tables on the basis of what is written there. While the advice contained there is sound and well researched and will, almost definitely, bring about performance improvements, this is not the way to do things. The ideas contained in the chapter can only serve as a guide and provide further food for thought.

It is altogether too easy to apply multiple changes to a system in the expectation that at least one, and hopefully a few, of the changes will cause things to get better. This is a frequently made mistake. It provides no way of being able to identify the contribution made to the overall improvement by each individual factor. More important, it is necessary to identify any changes that have no effect or have had a negative impact.

While good results can be achieved with this approach, the outcome would be even better if the changes had been applied in a more gradual and measured manner.

No Man Is an Island. Don't try to do anything in isolation — the days of the DP hero are well and truly over.

Having identified a problem or bottleneck, its resolution should be made on the basis of discussions with *all* interested parties. This may mean involving one or more of the following: the team responsible for application development, the MVS system team, the data management or data base administration group, operations, hardware planning, the network management team, or the end-users.

Listen *carefully* to any objections they might raise in response to your proposed changes. Unless you can counter these objections then you will have to re-focus your point of attack.

More Haste, Less Speed. Don't hurry. Again there is a temptation to plough headlong into the problem with scant regard for the consequences of your actions. Only by applying changes one at a time and by monitoring the effects of each single change can truly effective control over performance be administered. Of course this a slow (and sometimes painful) process, but remember: *slowly but surely wins the race.*

Sources of Further Information

Today's computing professional can hardly complain about the quantity of information available, much of which is free of charge. What *is* debatable is the quality of this material. A lot of it is written either as thinly veiled advertising copy or with the purpose of building or reenforcing the credentials of an industry guru. Little will be found in the computer press aimed directly at CICS users. IBM must be congratulated in making the *CICS Performance* manual such an excellent reference manual and a refreshing change from many of their other publications. Unfortunately, even at a price, good solid practical information is hard to come by.

In my work as the editor of *CICS Update*, I have found an eager audience for technical information on CICS, and I am sure this feeling could be echoed by other subscriber journals such as *The CICS Report* and *Performance Review*, and *The Candle Report*, which is distributed free. All try to give their readers the benefit of others' practical experiences, albeit in slightly different ways. All should be essential reading material for CICS systems programmers and performance analysts.

Understanding the idiosyncrasies of CICS performance is a lifetime's work. Try to gather as much information as you can from as many different sources as you can. Some of the information in this book was gathered from conversations with fellow delegates over lunch at user group meetings and technological seminars. It is amazing what can be learned for the price of a glass of beer!

Appendix

CICS DATA COMPRESION PACKAGES

BIMCMPRS

In the USA:

B I Moyle Associates, Inc.
5788 Lincoln Drive
Minneapolis, MN 55436
Telephone: (612) 933 2885

In the UK:

Interlogic Ltd.
Mawby House
28-32 Spittal Street
Marlow, Bucks SL7 1DB
Telephone: (06284) 73113

CICS/CPR

In the USA:

MacKinney Systems
Suite 112
2674-A South Glenstone
Springfield, MO 65804
Telephone: (417) 882 8012

In the UK:

Gerrard Data Systems
2 Orley Court
Greenford Road
Harrow, Middx HA1 3QD
Telephone: (01) 423 2277

CICS-WINDOWS

In the USA:

Softouch Systems, Inc.
8217 South Walker
Oklahoma City, OK 73139
Telephone: (405) 632 4745

CTOP AND CTOP III

In the USA:

H & W Computer Systems, Inc.
3166 Elder Street
Boise, ID 83715
Telephone: (208) 377 0336

In the UK:

Systems Resources (Midlands) Ltd.
Systems House
27 Spon Street
Coventry,Warwickshire CV1 3BA
Telephone: (0203) 26301

DATAPACKER

In the USA:

H & M Systems Software, Inc.
25 East Spring Valley Avenue
Maywood, NJ 07607-2120
Telephone: (201) 845 3357

In the UK:

H & M Systems Software
Waterwitch House
Exeter Road
Newmarket, Suffolk CB8 8LR
Telephone: (0638) 668683

OTTO/CICS

In the UK:

The European Software Company Ltd.
2nd Floor Waterford House
Denmark Street
Wokingham, Berks RG11 2YF
Telephone: (0990) 23491

PIE/CICS-DSO (DATA STREAM OPTIMIZER)

In the USA:

Technologic Software Concepts, Inc.
150 El Camino Real
Tustin, CA 92680
Telephone: (714) 730 1290

3270 SUPEROPTIMIZER FOR CICS

In the USA:

BMC Software, Inc.
P.O. Box 2002
Sugar Land, TX 77487-8800
Telephone: (713) 240 8800

In the UK:

BMC Software Ltd.
St Georges House
Knoll Road
Camberley, Surrey GU15 3SY
Telephone: (0276) 62653

CICS SOFTWARE PERFORMANCE MONITORS

ADR/IDEAL

In the USA:

Applied Data Research, Inc.
Route 206 and Orchard Road
CN-8
Princeton, NJ 08540
Telephone: (201) 874 9000

In the UK:

> Applied Data Research Ltd.
> Portmill House
> 37-40 Portmill Lane
> Hitchin, Herts SG5 1DJ
> Telephone: (0462) 55353

BEST/1- MVS (CICS Feature)

In the USA:

> BGS Systems, Inc.
> 128 Technology Center
> Waltham, MA 02254-9111
> Telephone: (617) 891 0000

In the UK:

> BGS Systems Ltd.
> Salisbury House
> Finsbury Circus
> London EC2M 5RH
> Telephone: (01) 588 0057

BIMODIS

In the USA:

> B I Moyle Associates, Inc.
> 5788 Lincoln Drive
> Minneapolis, MN 55436
> Telephone: (612) 933 2885

In the UK:

Interlogic Ltd.
Mawby House
28 Spittal Street
Marlow, Bucks SL9 7HG
Telephone: (06284) 71384

CA-JARS/CICS

In the USA:

Computer Associates International, Inc.
711 Stewart Avenue
Garden City, NY 11530-4787
Telephone: (516) 227 3300

In the UK:

Computer Associates Ltd.
183-187 Bath Road
Slough
Berks SL1 4AA
Telephone: (0753) 77733

CICS MANAGER

In the USA:

Boole and Babbage Inc.
510 Oakmead Parkway
Sunnyvale, CA 94086
Telephone: (408) 735 9550

In the UK:

> The European Software Company Ltd.
> 2nd Floor, Waterford House
> Denmark Street
> Wokingham, Berks RG11 2YF
> Telephone: (0990) 23491

CICSPARS

International Business Machines

Contact your local agent for further information

CICSPARS/MVS AND CICSPARS/VSE

International Business Machines

Contact your local agent for further information

EPILOG 1000 FOR CICS

In the USA:

> Candle Corporation
> 1999 Bundy Drive
> Los Angeles, CA 90025
> Telephone: (213) 442 4042

In the UK:

> Candle Service Ltd.
> Swan Gardens
> 3rd Floor
> 10 Piccadilly
> London W1V 9LA
> Telephone: (01) 734 8292

ESRA/CICS

In the USA:

Candle Corporation
1999 Bundy Drive
Los Angeles, CA 90025
Telephone: (213) 442 4042

In the UK:

Candle Service Ltd.
Swan Gardens
3rd Floor
10 Piccadilly
London W1V 9LA
Telephone: (01) 734 8292

EXPLORE/CICS

In the USA:

Goal Systems International Inc.
Goal Systems Building
5455 North High Street
Columbus, OH 43214-1193
Telephone: (614) 895 8500

In the UK:

Goal Systems International Ltd.
St Peter's House
2 Bricket Road
St Albans, Herts AL1 3JW
Telephone: (0727) 41241

MICS/CICS

In the USA:

Morino Associates Inc.
8615 Westwood Center Drive
Vienna, VA 22180-2215
Telephone: (703) 734 9494

In the UK:

Morino Associates (uk) Ltd.
103 St Peter Street
St Albans, Herts AL1 3EN
Telephone: (0727) 37464

THE MONITOR FOR CICS

In the USA:

Landmark Systems Corporation
8000 Towers Crescent Drive
Vienna, VA 22180-2700
Telephone (703) 893 9046

In the UK:

Systems Resources (Midlands) Ltd.
27 Spon Street
Coventry CV1 3BA
Telephone: (0203) 26301

OMEGAMON/CICS

In the USA:

Candle Corporation
1999 Bundy Drive
Los Angeles, CA 90025
Telephone: (213) 442 4042

In the UK:

Candle Service Ltd.
Swan Gardens
3rd Floor
10 Piccadilly
London W1V 9LA
Telephone: (01) 734 8292

PEEKCSA

In the USA:

MacKinney Systems
Suite 112
2674-A South Glenstone
Springfield, MO 65804
Telephone: (417) 882 8012

In the UK:

Gerrard Data Systems
2 Orley Court
Greenford Road
Harrow, Middx HA1 3QD
Telephone: (01) 423 2277

PILOT/CICS

In the USA:

Axios Products, Inc.
1455 Veterans Highway
Hauppage, NY 11788-4836
Telephone: (516) 348 1900

RTA/CICS

In the USA:

Candle Corporation
1999 Bundy Drive
Los Angeles, CA 90025
Telephone: (213) 442 4042

In the UK:

Candle Service Ltd.
Swan Gardens
3rd Floor
10 Piccadilly, London W1V 9LA
Telephone: (01) 734 8292

SNOOP FOR CICS

In the USA:

Interactive Solutions, Inc.
53 West Fort Lee Road
Bogota, NJ 07603
Telephone: (201) 488 3708

STROBE/CICS PERFORMANCE MEASUREMENT

In the USA:

Programart
30 Battle Street
Cambridge, MA 02138
(617) 661 3020

SYSTEM ACCOUNTING (REACT)

In the UK:

Macro 4 PLC
Crabbett Park House
Turners Hill Road
Crawley, West Sussex RH10 4SS
Telephone: (0293) 886060

In the USA:

Macro 4 Inc.
Millbrook Plaza
P.O. Box 187
Mount Freedom, NJ 07970
Telephone: (201) 895 4800

Bibliography

Anderson, WM, Balancing CICS response times, *CICS Update*, October 1987

Banister, John, Additional CICS system recovery table entry, *CICS Update*, October 1986

Banister, John, BMS — the DDS parameter, *CICS Update*, April 1987

Banister, John, CICS COBOL compile option tip, *CICS Update*, December 1987

Basford, Ian, CICS and 4GLs as system software, *CICS Update*, February 1986

Bryan, John, Concentrating reference patterns, *CICS Update*, June 1986

Bryan, John, VSAM performance in CICS, *CICS Update*, July 1986

Burton, Keith, Program isolation scheduling, *CICS Update*, January 1987

Buzen, Dr. Jeffrey, Capacity planning for hosts and networks, *Network Management*, May/June 1987

Clark, D.F., Optimising VSAM performance under CICS, *CICS Update*, June 1986

Clark, Katherine, VSAM tuning tips, *CICS Update*, May 1986

Coan, D.R., CICS problems in a high paging environment, *CICS Update*, January 1986

Coker, Stephen, Allocation of real storage in a VSE environment, *CICS Update*, August 1986

Czyz, Thomas, A problem with VSE BUFSIZE parameter, *CICS Update*, December 1985

Dawson, Richard, DL/I statistics and hardcopy, *CICS Update*, August 1986

Dean, Kevin, Improving the value of CICS, statistics, *CICS Update*, February 1986

Doerrler, Nadia, CICS COBOL programming guidelines, *CICS Update*, December 1985

Downes, Andrew, Hints and tips on PLT, *CICS Update*, January 1986

El-Imad, Jamil, CICS message routing, *CICS Update*, June 1987

Fry, Stephen, CICS/COBOL restricted words, *CICS Update*, May 1986

Glen, Kenneth, Suggested CICS Programming standards, *CICS Update*, January 1986

Hansen, Steen, Controlling CICS performance under VM/VSE, *CICS Update*, May 1988

Harper, Thomas, Writing your own terminal error program, *CICS Update*, February 1988

Harris D.J., The effect of bad key compression on a VSAM KSDS,
  CICS Update, October 1986

Hayward, Bob, CICS with IMS/DB, *CICS Performance*, Xephon 1987

IBM CICS/VS 1.6 Performance Guide SC33-0134

IBM CICS/VS 1.7 Customization Guide SC33-0239

IBM CICS/VS 1.7 Facilities and Planning Guide SC33-0202

IBM CICS/VS 1.7 Installation and Operations Guide SC33-0071

IBM CICS/VS 1.7 Performance Guide SC33-0229

IBM CICS/VS 1.7 Performance Data SC33-0212

IBM CICS/VS 1.7 Release Guide GC33-0132

IBM CICS/VS 1.7 Resource Definition (Online) SC33-0186

IBM CICS/VS 1.7 Resource Definition (Macro) SC33-0237

IBM Data Stream Device Guide SC33-0233

Jatich, Alida, Preventing CICS system crashes and lock-outs, *CICS
  Update*, May 1987

Jatich, Alida, CICS HANDLE versus RESP/RESP2, *CICS Update*,
  November 1987

Joehlin, Gary, CICS methodology, *CICS Performance*, Xephon 1987

Jones, Mike, A problem with CICS dynamic storage, *CICS Update*,
  March 1986

Jones, Graham, DL/I and CICS, *CICS Performance*, Xephon 1987

Krynicki, Joe, Defining VSAM files with IMBED, *CICS Update*,
    September 1987

Lee, Robert, Auto-install terminal-id assignment, *CICS Update*,
    December 1987

le Noir, Thomas and Cummings, Constance, Tuning VSAM to
    recover space, *CICS Update*, December 1987

Lewis, Graeme, GETVIS problems in CICS, *CICS Update*, October
    1986

Lindstrom, Scott, Deadly embraces/VSAM strings, *CICS Update*,
    April 1986

Logan, Derrick, Tuning on-line VSAM files, *CICS Update*,
    September 1986

Lowe, Doug, *CICS for the COBOL Programmer*, Parts 1 and 2, Mike
    Murach and Associates Inc 1984

Lyszyk, Mike, Application design/CICS performance, *CICS
    Performance*, Xephon 1987

Maltz, Melvyn, Program residency, *CICS Update*, May 1986

Manley, Donna, CICS GETVIS problems, *CICS Update*, April 1986

Marquardt, Kenneth, CICS tuning parameters, *CICS Update*,
    January 1988

McConnell, Phil, SRM parameters, *MVS Performance*, Xephon 1987

McCrary, Charles, CMF Performance, *CICS Update*, December 1985

McDonald, Thomas, Controls for wider reach, *Computerworld*,
    February 2 1987

Mead, Philip, CICS system parameters, *CICS Performance*, Xephon 1987

Mead, Philip, CICS virtual storage, *CICS Performance*, Xephon 1987

Meier, Klaus, Balancing CICS response times, *CICS Update*, June 1987

Myllyniemi, Kari, Speeding up CICS program loads, *CICS Update*, September 1986

Nisenson, Pinchas, How to improve CICS program loads, *CICS Update*, March 1987

Noll, Erich, Tuning IMS/DB VSAM buffer pools for CICS, *CICS Update*, January 1988

Northcote, Scott, Keeping remote BTAM lines in service, *CICS Update*, September-October 1987

Ozaniec, Jerry, CICS/VS application design, *CICS Performance*, Xephon 1987

Payne, Graham, CICS abending with U0203, *CICS Update*, June 1986

Performance Review, Reducing CICS memory requirements, June 1987

Performance Review, Global CICS performance parameters, July-August 1987

Pearkins, John, CICS performance in VSE, *CICS Update*, March 1986

Potter, Kevin, Using XPCCB macros, *CICS Update*, September 1987

Ranade, Jay, *VSAM Performance, Design, and Fine Tuning* MacMillan Publishing Co 1987

Reiss, Avraham, A self-tuning system, *CICS Update*, April 1987

Rivington, Mark, CICS Performance — a general overview, *CICS Performance*, Xephon 1987

Schaal, Alfred, The performance implications of PUTSPOOL, GETSPOOL, and CTLSPOOL, *CICS Update*, October 1986

Technology Transfer SARL, Les moniteurs on-line CICS, *Technology Transfer SARL* 1987

The CICS Report, Efficient CICS programs, July 1986

The CICS Report, VSAM deadlocks, September 1986

The CICS Report, VSAM Local Shared Resources, December 1986

The CICS Report, Minimizing program compression, January 1987

The CICS Report, Locate vs. move mode processing, February 1987

The CICS Report, Efficient sceen handling, August 1987

The CICS Report, More on efficient data communications, September 1987

The CICS Report, The pitfalls of EIBRESP, October 1987

Tomlinson, Ed, More GETVIS problems, *CICS Update*, August 1986

van der Pol, Walther, LSR considerations, *CICS Update*, February 1988

Vanwesemael, Michel, Stabilising CICS response times, *CICS Update*, November 1986

von Weisz, Bjorn, Tuning DL/I buffers in CICS, *CICS Update*, December 1987

Williams, John, Virtual storage constraint relief (CICS), *CICS Update*, February 1986

Xephon, *3270 Handbook*, Xephon 1987

Xephon, *CICS in Practice*, Xephon 1984

Xephon, *CICS in Action*, Xephon 1985

Xephon, *Software Performance Monitors*, Xephon 1987

Xephon, *VM Performance in Practice*, Xephon 1986

Yelavich, B.M., Customer Information Control System — An evolving system facility, *IBM Systems Journal*, Vol 24 Nos 3/4 1985

Glossary

Abend — The abnormal termination of a program or task caused by an error condition.

Access method — The means by which data is transferred between main storage and peripheral devices. The principal access methods found in CICS environments are VSAM, VTAM, BTAM, and TCAM.

Active Maximum Tasks (AMXT) — A threshold defined in the SIT which limits the number of tasks that may be dispatched by CICS at any given time.

Active task — A task that is not waiting for the completion of an event and which is eligible for dispatching.

Activity keypoint — The information recorded on the system log to facilitate a possible emergency restart. There are two types of activity keypoint: system activity keypoints, which are written automatically by CICS and user activity keypoints, which are under the control of the user.

AID — See Automatic Initiate Descriptor.

AKPFREQ — An SIT parameter used to specify the frequency with which activity keypoints are recorded. This frequency determines the length of time any subsequent emergency restart will take.

ALT — See Application Load Table.

AMXT — See Active Maximum Tasks.

Application Load Table (ALT) — A CICS table used to define the order in which resident modules and maps are to be loaded into virtual storage at system initialization time.

ATI — See Automatic Transaction Initiation.

Automatic Initiate Descriptor (AID) — A CICS control block used to control the execution of automatically-initiated tasks.

Automatic Transaction Initiation (ATI) — The automatic invocation of a transaction associated with an entry in the DCT on reaching a user- defined trigger level.

Auxiliary temporary storage — Temporary storage queues held on the VSAM data set DFHTEMP as opposed to being held in main storage.

Basic Mapping Support (BMS) — An interface between CICS and an application program to control the movement and presentation of data streams to and from a terminal.

Basic Telecommunications Access Method (BTAM) — an old, but still very much alive, terminal access method lacking a lot of the functionality of VTAM.

BMS — See Basic Mapping Support.

Browsing — The sequential processing of a data set.

BTAM — See Basic Telecommunications Access Method.

Buffer — An area of virtual storage used to process data which normally resides on a external device (eg DASD, display terminal etc).

BUFND — An FCT parameter used to specify the number of data buffers to be allocated to a VSAM data set.

BUFNI — An FCT parameter used to specify the number of index buffers to be allocated to a VSAM data set.

CEBR — An IBM-supplied transaction used to browse temporary storage queues on-line.

CECI — An IBM-supplied transaction used to interactively execute CICS command-level program instructions.

CEDA — An IBM-supplied transaction used to perform Resource Definition On-line operations.

CEDF — An IBM-supplied transaction used as a programming tool to debug CICS applications.

CEMT — An IBM-supplied transaction used to monitor and control CICS resources.

CEST — An IBM-supplied transaction providing a subset of CEMT functions.

CESN — An IBM-supplied sign-on transaction.

Class Maximum Tasks (CMXT) — A threshold defined in the SIT which limits the number of tasks for any of up to ten different classes of transaction which may be in the system at any given time.

CMSG — An IBM-supplied message switching transaction.

CMXT — See Class Maximum Tasks.

Command-level — A method of CICS appliaction programming that uses the EXEC CICS ... END EXEC format. An easier method of programming than macro-level, which it has largely replaced.

COMMAREA — An area available to command-level programs used to pass data between tasks in pseudo-conversational mode or between programs within the same task.

Common System Area (CSA) — The major CICS control block containing pointers, either directly or indirectly, to all others.

Control Area — The unit of space allocation for a VSAM data set. Each control area comprises a number of control intervals. VSAM selects an 'appropriate' size for a Control Area based on how space is defined for the data set.

Control Area split — The action of dividing one Control Area into two. Control Area splits occur when there is insufficient freespace in a Control Area to add new records. These can have a serious impact on performance.

Control Interval — The unit of data transfer for a VSAM data set, independent of the physical record size. Control Interval size may be defined explicitly using IDCAMS or allowed to default, in which case VSAM will select a 'suitable' value based on the data set's record size, device type, and buffer space.

Control Interval split — The action of dividing one Control Interval into two. Control Interval splits occur when there is insufficient freespace in a Control Interval to add new records. These can effect performance.

Conversational program — A CICS program which maintains control of its resources throughout its life even when waiting for a response from the terminal.

CICS Monitoring Facility (CMF) — A optional component of CICS for the recording and collection of CICS-related performance data.

CICS System Definition (CSD) file — The data set used by CICS to retain information on resources which are defined using the RDO facility.

CMF — See CICS Monitoring facility.

CSA — See Common System Area.

CSD file — See CICS System Definition file.

CSTT — An IBM-supplied transaction used to control the collection of CICS run-time statistics.

Data stream — The amount of data transmitted to or from a terminal in one read or write operation.

Data Management Block (DMB) — A DL/I control block which represents the logical definition of a DL/I data base.

DCA — See Dispatch Control Area.

DCT — See Destination Control Table.

Deadlock — A potentially unending situation where one task is waiting for resources held by another task which in turn is waiting for resources held by the first task.

Dequeue — The process of a task relinquishing exclusive control over a resource making it available to other tasks.

Destination Control Table (DCT) — A CICS table used to hold transient data destination definitions.

Dispatch — The process of making the CPU available to a task awaiting execution.

Dispatch Control Area (DCA) — A CICS control block holding priority and status information of a task. The DCA is used to control the execution of tasks in a CICS system.

DFHPEP — Program Error Program. An optional user-coded module which is given control by CICS whenever a task abends.

DFHTEP — Terminal Error Program. An optional user-coded module which is given control by CICS whenever an unrecoverable terminal I/O error occurs.

Dial-up line — A data transmission facility using a public telephone line. Also called a switched line.

DMB — See Data Management Block.

DSA — See Dynamic Storage Area.

DTB — See Dynamic Transaction Backout.

Dynamic Storage Area (DSA) — An area of CICS storage that is divided into seven subpools (program subpool, control subpool, shared subpool, isolated subpool, mixed subpool, teleprocessing subpool, and RPL subpool), and which is continuously being allocated and freed by CICS applications and sometimes CICS itself.

Dynamic Transaction Backout (DTB) — The cancellation of changes made to a protected resource in the event of a task abending.

Enqueue — A request for the exclusive control of a resource. If the resource is available, the task will continue: otherwise, the task will be placed on the suspended chain.

FCT — See File Control Table.

File Control Table (FCT) — A CICS table used to hold data set definitions.

Forward recovery — The process of applying recorded updates to a previous copy of a data set in order to restore it to its current status.

GETVIS — The amount of virtual storage left in a VSE partition once the amount of storage specified in the SIZE parameter of the EXEC statement has been allocated. GETVIS is used extensively for VSAM buffers and by VSAM itself.

Help Desk — A section of the Data Processing department offering itself as the first point of contact for end users experiencing hardware or software malfunctions.

ICV — The partition exit time interval. A parameter in the SIT used to specify the amount of time CICS will relinquish control to the operating system should it find no work to run.

IVCR — The runaway task time interval. A parameter in the SIT used to specify the amount of time that may elapse from the issuing of a CICS command after which CICS will deem the task to have 'run away' and will issue an AICA abend.

ICVS — The system stall time interval. A parameter in the SIT used to specify the amount of time CICS will wait before abending tasks defined as SPURGE=YES in the PCT after it has detected a 'stress' situation.

ICVSWT — The VSE short wait time interval. A parameter in the SIT used to specify the amount of time for which CICS will relinquish control to VSE while it waits for the completion of a short wait (eg completion of a disk I/O).

ICVTSD — The terminal scan delay time interval. A parameter in the SIT used to specify the frequency between each attempt by CICS to process requests for terminal output. ICE — See Interval Control Element.

IDCAMS — The VSAM batch utility program.

Intent scheduling — A DL/I facility which restricts the ability to update a data base to one task at a time. With intent scheduling, the task enqueues upon the appropriate PSB.

Intersystem Communication (ISC) — A mechanism, using SNA facilities, by which CICS address spaces and partitions in different CPUs can communicate and share resources.

Interval Control Element (ICE) — A CICS control block used to control time-dependent CICS requests.

ISC — See Intersystem Communication.

JCT — See Journal Control Table.

Journal Control Table (JCT) — A CICS control table used to hold journal data set definitions.

Journalling — The recording of changes made to CICS data sets to facilitate forward recovery.

LINK — A CICS command which allows two CICS programs to be connected. The 'linking' program will resume processing from its next sequential instruction when the 'linked to' program has completed.

Link Pack Area (LPA) — An area of virtual storage in MVS containing re-entrant modules which can be used concurrently by other address spaces.

LOAD — A CICS command which loads a program into storage controlled by another CICS program.

Local device — A device whose control unit is attached directly to a mainframe's data channel and not via a telecommunications line.

Local Shared Resources (LSR) — The sharing of a common buffer pool by multiple VSAM data sets.

Locate mode I/O — A method of processing files which uses the actual addresses of records in VSAM buffers.

Look-aside — A file read which CICS is able to process using data already in its buffers and thus which does not require any physical I/O.

LPA — See Link Pack Area.

LSR — See Local Shared Resources.

Macro-level — A method of CICS application programming that uses DFH..macros to interface with CICS. A much more complex and cumbersome method than command-level.

Main temporary storage — A temporary storage queue held in main storage as opposed to being held on an auxiliary data set.

Map — The program's representation of a screen display or printed page.

Maximum number of tasks (MXT) — A threshold defined in the SIT which limits the number of tasks that may be present (not necessarily active) in the system at any given time.

Message switching — The process of directing messages to one or more terminals over a data network.

Move mode I/O — A method of processing files where records are loaded into the working storage of the program.

MRO — See Multi-region Operation.

Multi-region Operation (MRO) — A mechanism by which different CICS address spaces and partitions within the same CPU can communicate and share resources.

MXT — See Maximum number of tasks.

NCP — See Network Control Program.

Network Control Program (NCP) — A user-generated program using definitions of the network which controls the running of a communications controller.

NLT — See Nucleus Load Table.

Non-switched line — A data transmission facility using a dedicated line between two fixed points on a network.

Nucleus — The part of a CICS address space or partition which contains the main CICS modules, control tables, and storage for resident programs.

Nucleus Load Table (NLT) — A CICS table used to define the order in which modules are to be loaded into the CICS nucleus at system initialization time.

Page Allocation Map (PAM) — A CICS control area used by the Storage Control Program to control the allocation and deallocation of areas of the DSA.

PAM — See Page Allocation Map.

PCB — See Program Communication Block.

PCT — See Program Control Table.

PL/I Shared Library facility — A facility which provides the ability to share routines between different CICS-PL/I programs.

PLT — See Program Load Table.

Polling — The interrogation of terminals by a terminal access method to determine their readiness to send or receive data.

PPT — See Processing Program Table.

Processing Program Table (PPT) — A CICS table used to hold application programs and map definitions.

Program Communication Block (PCB) — A DL/I control block used to control access to a data base's segments.

Program compression — The deletion of non-resident programs from the DSA when insufficient storage is available for further processing.

Program Control Table (PCT) — A CICS table used to hold transaction definitions.

Program isolation — A DL/I facility which restricts the ability to update a data base to one task at a time. Program isolation causes a task to enqueue upon an individual segment and its dependent segments.

Program List Table (PLT) — A CICS table used to hold a list of user programs that are to be executed immediately after CICS has been initialized (PLTPI) or at CICS shut-down (PLTSD).

Program Specification Block (PSB) — A DL/I control block comprised of one or more PCBs.

PRTY — A VSE operator command used to define the order of priority in which VSE partitions are to be dispatched.

PSB — See Program Specification Block.

Pseudo-conversational program — One of a series of CICS programs which simulates a continuous dialogue but which, in reality, relinquishes the control of its resources at each terminal interaction.

QEA — See Queue Element Area.

Queue Element Area (QEA) — A CICS control block used to enqueue upon a resource.

RDO — See Resource Definition On-line.

Real storage — Storage for which there is a direct one-for-one relationship with the physically available storage of the processor.

Reference set — The amount of real storage necessary to sustain the processing of the commonest applications without causing any paging.

Remote device — A device whose control unit is attched to CICS via a telecommunications line and not directly through a mainframe's data channel.

Resident program — A program or map loaded into the CICS nucleus so that it is kept permanently in main storage and not paged out.

Resource — A program, file, transient data queue, or temporary storage queue which is available for a CICS transaction to use.

Resource Definition On-Line (RDO) — A CICS facility for defining certain resources on-line via the CEDA transaction rather than assembling tables.

Response time — The length of time taken between entering data and receiving a reply. Internal response time (ie the view that CICS has of the task) is a fraction of the actual response time (ie the terminal operator's view of the task).

SAA — See Storage Accounting Area.

SCS — See Storage Cushion Size.

Service Level Agreement (SLA) — A document which defines a measurable commitment by the Data Processing department in respect of its supply oi computer services to an end user.

Shared Virtual Area (SVA) — An area of virtual storage in VSE containing re-entrant modules which can be used concurrently by multiple VSE partitions.

Short-on-Storage (SOS) — The status of CICS when it has not been able to satisfy a request for storage even by performing program compression.

Sign-on-Table (SNT) — A CICS table used to hold terminal operator and related authorization definitions.

SIT — See System Initialization Table.

SLA — See Service Level Agreement.

SNT — See Sign-on Table.

SOS — See Short-on-Storage.

SPURGE — A PCT parameter used to indicate whether a transaction can be purged from the system in the event of CICS entering a 'stress' situation.

SRT — See System Recovery Table.

Storage Cushion Size (SCS) — The amount of storage defined in the SIT used to satisfy requests for storage which could not be met by performing program compression.

Storage Accounting Area (SAA) — An indicator at the beginning of each storage area identifying what type of storage it is.

String — One of a number of sets of buffers allowing concurrent access to a data set by multiple users. The number of strings is defined in the STRNO parameter of the FCT.

SVA — See Shared Virtual Area.

Syncpoint — A point in the life of a task when updates to recoverable resources are committed.

System Initialization Table (SIT) — A CICS table used to hold system information which is used by CICS at system start-up time.

System Recovery Table (SRT) — A CICS table used to hold abend or abnormal condition codes which CICS is to intercept.

Task — The unit of work associated with the processing of a single transaction.

Task Control Area (TCA) — The major control block of a task, lasting throughout its life, and contolling its execution.

TCA — See Task Control Area.

TCAM — See Telecommunications Access Method.

TCT — See Terminal Control Table.

Telecommunication Access Method (TCAM) — A terminal access method that enables application programs to access devices as if they were sequential files.

Temporary storage — A scratchpad facility in CICS allowing data to be easily transferred within programs. Temporary storage is seldom temporary.

Temporary Storage Table (TST) — A CICS table used to hold details of recoverable temporary storage queues.

Terminal Control Table (TCT) — A CICS table used to hold terminal definitions.

Terminal Input Output Area (TIOA) — A CICS control area used in the transfer of data to and from a terminal.

TIOA — See Terminal Input Output Area.

TPBAL — A VSE operator command used to define the number of partitions that can be suspended should an excessive paging rate be experienced.

Transaction — An operation that takes place as the result of a single terminal request. Multiple users can initiate the same transaction.

Transient data — Data written sequentially to a queue (intra-partition or extra-partition) specified in the DCT. Transient data can only be read once by a CICS application.

Transaction List Table (XLT) — A CICS table used to hold the names of transactions which are to be allowed to execute during the first quiesce stage of a controlled shut-down.

TST — See Temporary Storage Table.

User exit — A point in an IBM-supplied program where control may be given to a user-written routine.

VIO — See Virtual Input Output.

Virtual Input Output (VIO) — An MVS method of I/O using system paging routines for data transfer.

Virtual storage — The theoretical amount of storage directly addressable by a program.

Virtual Storage Access Method (VSAM) — An access method for the direct, sequential, or key-sequenced processing of files stored on DASD.

Virtual Telecommunication Access Method (VTAM) — A high-function terminal access method, which runs independently of CICS in its own address space or partition.

VSAM — See Virtual Storage Access Method.

VTAM — See Virtual Telecommunications Access Method.

XCTL — A CICS command which allows control to be passed from one program to another at the same logical level with no provision for returning to the original program.

XLT — See Transaction List Table.

Index